CULTURE CLASH

EVOLUTION OF AN EXPAT

BENJAMIN LONG

Vince, 1/6/17

Stay evolutionary my friend.

"Culture Clash: Evolution of an Expat," by Benjamin Long, ISBN 978-1-62137-796-2 (hardcover); ISBN 978-1-62137-763-4 (softcover); ISBN 978-1-62137-764-1 (eBook).

Published 2015 by Virtualbookworm.com Publishing Inc., P.O. Box 9949, College Station, TX 77842, US.

© 2017, Benjamin Long. All rights reserved. No part of this publication may be reproduced, stored in a retrieval system, or transmitted in any form or by any means, electronic, mechanical, recording or otherwise, without the prior written permission of Benjamin Long.

To the memory of my grandmother

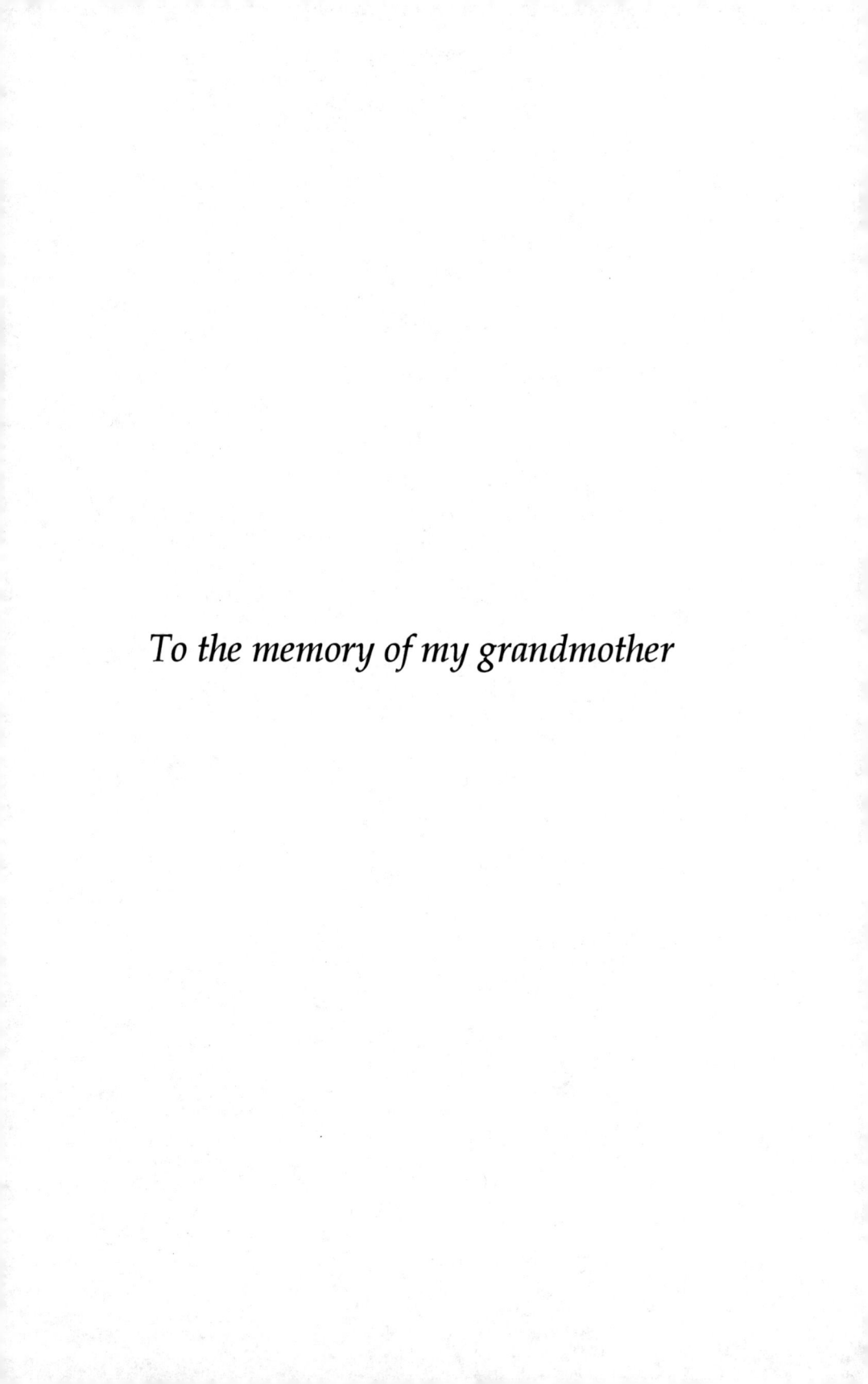

CONTENTS

Part - I: Cultural Core, Norms & Gestures 1
   1 It's Only Cultural Not Personal 3

Part - II: My Initial Cultural Conditioning 23
   2 The Dichotomy Of Absolute Poverty 25
   3 Sacrifices And Consequences 37
   4 Love, Give, And Forgive 51
   5 The Looming Change 75

Part – III: Unlearning My Deeply Held Beliefs 97
   6 A Strange New World 99
   7 The Dark Side Of Unconditional Love 125
   8 Beyond The Limits Of Fear 161
   9 Knowledge Is Power 181

Part– IV: Changed Perceptions Modified Actions 201
   10 Fading Cultural Codes 203
   11 The Consummate Underdog 233
   12 Evolve: The Man I've Become 249

PART - I

CULTURAL CORE, NORMS & GESTURES

CHAPTER 1

IT'S ONLY CULTURAL, NOT PERSONAL: MAKING SENSE OF THE CULTURAL FOG

"Each of us has his or her distinctive personality. But overlaid on top of that are tendencies and assumptions and reflexes handed down to us by the history of the community we grew up in, and those differences are extraordinarily specific."

- Malcolm Gladwell

***

"Why do Filipinos point with their lips?"

My colleague, Mark asked casually as he sat across from me at a restaurant during an office lunch break. Admittedly, I was a little annoyed by his question and thought he was making fun of my ethnicity. *What an odd thing to say*, I thought. I couldn't make out if he was trying to be insulting, or was just plain stupid. I had known Mark for some time and considered him a fair and respectful man.

I said, "That's ridiculous! Filipinos don't point with their lips. That's the silliest thing I've ever heard you say, Mark!"

I completely brushed his question off, and he wisely let it go. As we waited for the waiter to take our orders, a very attractive woman who entered the restaurant caught my eye.

Trying to be discreet, I leaned forward and said quietly to Mark, "Don't be too obvious, but check her out."

"Where?" he asked.

With my lips puckered out in the direction of the woman, I whispered, "Over there!"

I caught myself pointing with my lips and immediately thought, *Oh boy, Mark was right. I am pointing with my lips!*

He didn't waste any time and started laughing hysterically while pointing at my directionally protruding lips. "See! I told you so!"

This little episode became the catalyst that sparked my interest in rediscovering and learning more of my Filipino heritage. I felt bad for harboring a negative reaction to Mark's observation, which had turned out to be accurate. I felt foolish for being unaware of this particular Filipino quirk that he had picked up on. It made me curious as to what other odd habits or behaviors I unknowingly displayed. A trip down memory lane made me realize that I often did things that might seem strange by Western standards.

After the lip-pointing incident heightened my curiosity, I was motivated to visit the Philippines more frequently to reconnect with my roots. I learned that lip-pointing comes from the Filipino culture's unfavorable view of pointing one's finger at anyone. As children, we were always reminded by elders that, "For every finger that you use to point at someone, four others are pointed at you."

Hence, to avoid any offences, lip-pointing was a politer alternative.

I continued to gain a better understanding of my quirks as I made regular visits to the Philippines through the years. Every time I visited, I rediscovered something new. It eventually became clear to me that all my seemingly odd behaviors were only cultural, and not personal. I felt a sense of relief in knowing that the peculiar things I did were considered perfectly normal in the Philippines.

I recall another culturally driven episode at my workplace. Unlike the lighthearted first example, this one could have adversely impacted my career. In 2004, my supervisor asked me to write my own performance evaluation. I didn't understand why he wanted me to write it; maybe he thought he was doing me a favor, or perhaps he was just too lazy to do it himself.

Because of my personal view of self-promotion at that time, the whole idea bothered me to such an extent that I opted to take the humble approach and downgrade my performance evaluation - rating myself a 3 out of 5. My line of thinking was that when my supervisor read what I had written, he would surely disagree with it and make the necessary changes.

Unfortunately, what actually transpired was not even close to what I had envisioned. When I submitted my performance evaluation, my supervisor signed it off and submitted it to the General Manager without reading it. A month later, I was in front of the big boss asking for a pay raise, and my general manager flatly said, "Ben, I was not very impressed with your last performance evaluation. In fact, I have a copy of it right here."

He pulled out what I had written for myself a month earlier and waved it in my face. The incident confused me tremendously because I genuinely believed that I had done the right thing by being humble, and was chastised instead.

Since migrating to America, my life had been a long series of these types of episodes. I often found myself doing things that were out of step with everyone else. Apparently, there was a huge disconnect somewhere that I'd yet to figure out. It would take many years for me to gain a solid understanding of the power and significance of cultural differences.

From the start, I wish someone had taken the time to compare the American and Philippine cultures and their differences. Even a basic understanding of these disparities would have saved me years of misunderstandings. If I had known it was only cultural, I probably wouldn't have taken my struggle personally or thought of myself as strange for seeing things so differently.

Unfortunately, I had to figure things out on my own as I went along. It would take decades of experience with American customs to find my footing. There was a lot of trial and error. Some lessons I learned quickly, and others took a very long time. It also did not help that, for so long, I held on to self-imposed barriers that prevented me from seeing the adverse impact cultural differences can bring.

One particular barrier that I created for myself was the illusion that cultural differences simply did not exist between the Philippines and United States. I spent years living under the impression that Filipinos were the same as Americans. My false notion was reinforced when I had to take a cultural awareness class in the Philippines as part of the immigration requirements to come to the United States. In retrospect, the class was useless because the instructor did not seem to realize that their even were cultural differences. Perhaps it was because he had never lived or visited the United States. The class mostly focused on the difference in climate. All I can recall is his repetitive warning, "Bundle up! It's going to be very cold in America."

Unfortunately, the course did not come close to even scratching the surface of the subject's potential depth. It only strengthened my naive conviction that cultural differences did not exist between us. The class did not give me the slightest hint of the rude awakening I would get in America. I would eventually learn about the existence of cultural differences, but it would be the hard way.

I also went through a denial phase. Unwilling to adapt to cultural changes, I deluded myself in thinking it was the Americans who needed to change, and not me. I didn't know any better and was foolish enough to try to convert everyone around me to see the wisdom of the Filipino ways. It was analogous to a fresh water fish that made his way to the open sea and tried to convince the salt water sea creatures that fresh water was best. In due course, I discovered what a waste of time and emotional drain that was.

Harry Truman once said, "How many times do you have to get hit in the head, before you figure out who is hitting you in the head?"

I eventually came to my senses and accepted the fact that I don't have the privilege to change the rules at my convenience. Culture makes its own rules; I just live in it. The adaption to a whole new culture was one of the most difficult tasks I had to endure, because it required for me to fundamentally rewire what I had already learned, embraced, and believed in.

Coming to terms with cultural differences made me realize and appreciate the abundance of various ethnic communities situated in major cities throughout the world. In Los Angeles alone, there are cultural enclaves like Chinatown, Korea Town, and Little Armenia, just to name a few. I now understand that these places provide a familiar environment to immigrants who are struggling to cope with the challenges to their cultural identity. It might have been helpful for me to have had a strong Filipino community where I lived, but in the 1970's, there were hardly any Filipinos living in Fontana, California. I was completely cut off from the world I knew and was thrown into mainstream American culture.

But of all the challenges I encountered in my struggle to understand cultural differences, the one that proved to be most difficult had to do with organizing. For me, trying to make sense of cultural differences on my own was like putting together a jigsaw puzzle without the benefit of seeing the puzzles' picture outside the box. I simply did not know how to process or make sense of the puzzling cultural divide I encountered frequently. It was incumbent upon me to come up with a way to sort-out and make some sense out of all these confusions.

It would take decades through trial and error before I was able to develop an organized way of looking at the subject matter rationally. The breakthrough for me was when I came up with a method to compartmentalize what I've learned and observed about cultural differences into three connecting parts. In doing so, I was able to organize, manage, and make sense of cultural differences in a coherent way; the nuts and bolts of how they differ, and most importantly – why?

To help illustrate this breakthrough, I will draw on the structural composition of a fruit as a model. If we were to take a fruit, let's say a mango, and diagonally slice it in half, we would see that it consists of three parts: the seed at the center, followed by the fruit itself, and the skin at its outer layer.

The seed, situated at its core, is a fundamental element of the fruit for it contains nature's secret ingredients for a mango's creation. However, as significant as the seed may be, it is invisible when the mango is viewed in its solid form - but we know that deep within its core - it exists. Similarly, a culture also contains a seed that holds the key to what makes each one unique. I refer to this seed as the "Cultural Core."

I view the cultural core as the governing principle that lies at the heart of every culture. It's the dominant force that shapes our values, behaviors, and moral codes. To briefly use another metaphor, it's the fuel that powers the engine of the cultural machine. For the Philippines, "collectivism" is the fuel that ignites its core.

Deep within the Filipino culture is the belief that the good of the many outweighs the good of any individual. So in this context, life is defined by one's relationship to the group. In a collective society, decisions are made with utmost thought to how the final outcome will impact the well-being of the family, relatives, friends, or community. Early on, I was conditioned to believe that what mattered most was the welfare of others.

If I had to list the names of the important people in my life, as a Filipino, I would be expected to write my name somewhere below, or maybe even at the bottom. If I were to deviate from this sacred rule by placing my name at the top, I would be deemed selfish. In a collective environment, society would subtly let me know that such an act was unacceptable and would then quietly guide me back into conformity.

While the Philippine cultural core is firmly anchored on the idea of group unity, in stark contrast, the American cultural core is solely based on "individualism."

It's a governing principle that favors the free action of individuals being self-reliant. In America, individual rights are so important that they are actually guaranteed in the First Amendment of the U.S. Constitution. In an Individualist society, individuals make decisions based on what is in their best interests. The impact a decision might have on other people is of secondary consequence. Americans are fiercely independent, and they believe the individual is responsible for his or her own success or failure. In this framework, I would be expected to write my name in the number one spot of my priority list. The logic behind this idea is, *How can I help others if I can't even help myself first?*

From a cultural core's perspective, it's easy to see how contradictory the two cultures really are; leaving plenty of room for conflicts and misunderstandings. This was a significant cultural shift. It was huge. My not knowing this from the start contributed greatly to the ripple effect of confusion and difficulty I encountered in my journey to cultural assimilation.

To go further to my mango analogy, the fruit itself, which lies between the seed and the skin, is distinguishable from any other fruit by virtue of its taste, texture, and smell. This portion of the fruit can be compared to the unique ways we conduct ourselves in accordance to our cultural traits. How we behave, our value system, and the way we view life makes us different from other cultures. This is what distinguishes the Philippines as a nation of Filipinos from the United States, a nation of Americans. I refer to these traits as the "Cultural Norms."

On the surface, the link between our value system, "Cultural Core," and the way we behave, "Cultural Norms," may seem obvious. However, connecting the relationships of these two dots into a comprehensive flow, which eluded me at first, took decades to figure out. For example during my early years in the United States, I was awestruck by the Americans' ability to say exactly what was on their mind, get right to the point, and act like it was no big deal. An American, for example, can easily say, "I disagree with you, and here's the reason why."

I found this behavior fascinating because it was something that I had difficulty doing. Coming from a collective society, I was conditioned to always be polite, keep things inside, and not make any waves. Consequently, I was not very good at communicating how I really felt or what I really wanted. Instead I mastered the art of dropping hints, and struggled with expressing my honest thoughts and opinions. I only found the courage to really say what I felt when things got too bottled up inside, to a point it could no longer be contained. But by then, what I blurted out was emotionally charged; coming across angry and mean.

This is why being "frank" has a negative connotation in Filipino culture, because we associate it with aggressive behavior. We have a saying in the Philippines that there are only three types of people that "frankly" tell the truth: a child, a drunk, and an angry person.

Whenever I was asked a direct question, in my attempt to give a polite response, I would be inclined to beat around the bush, usually just lapsing into an analysis of the problem rather than giving a real answer. My American friends found it annoying.

By connecting the cultural core and norms together, a picture emerged that explained why Americans are excellent communicators and why I struggled. Having been raised in the Philippines, I was conditioned to fit the mold of the Collectivist core principle, just as an American child is brought up to thrive in an Individualistic society. In all cultures, conditioning begins at home with the child's most powerful authority figure, parents.

In America, children are taught right from the start to always speak their mind and question authority. In the countless hours I spent dining with my American friends and their families, I observed and was amazed by the way lessons could be passed on to children in the span of a simple meal.

My American friends encouraged their children to have an open dialogue with them at the dinner table. The kids were constantly reminded to speak up if they had any doubts, or if they weren't clear about something. They were also encouraged to find things out for themselves and not just take someone's word for it. Furthermore, my American friends would nod encouragingly, cheer, and applaud when their kids made a good point. As part of their Individualist cultural makeup, American kids are taught that their opinions matter.

In contrast, Filipino children are conditioned to be obedient, mindful, and respectful of authority. A parent's decision or opinion is non-negotiable and should never be questioned. To question a parent's authority, especially in the presence of others, is considered an intolerable sign of disrespect.

Typically, a parent will warn a child with a disapproving look. Those who do not heed the warning and persist are then scolded, or even spanked. I learned early on that if Mom said the sky was green, out of respect, I was not going to argue with her. Parents' right to exert their influence on the lives of their children is a lifelong entitlement. Even in adulthood, a parent's approval or disapproval of a friend or significant other can make or break a relationship. A Collective society believes that obedience is the highest form of virtue.

A similar rule is applied to other authority figures, such as teachers. The Filipino school system is monologue-based - teachers talk, and good students listen quietly and take notes. If they are listening attentively, they should not have any questions. In my day, teachers were allowed to physically reprimand students who misbehaved. They could throw erasers at students, have them stand in the corner of the room, pinch them, and even whip them with a stick, all to keep students in line.

I was blown away when I first attended an American Catholic school in the eighth grade and watched a student openly disagree with a teacher, who happened to be a nun. Through my Collectivist set of eyes, I thought the student had behaved disrespectfully. I was further surprised to see that despite the seemingly relentless arguments that took place during class, teachers never physically reprimanded their students to get their points across. Points were made by way of verbal expression and the strength of each argument.

If, at an early stage, children are taught to overcome the fear of questioning the most powerful authority figure in their lives, they will then naturally grow up having no hesitation voicing what's on their mind to anyone. Americans are excellent at verbally expressing how they feel, because it's ingrained in them early on.

In contrast, I was taught to subordinate how I felt and to never challenge figures of authority. I was sold on the idea that the preservation of group cohesiveness and showing silent respect to authority figures was more important than self-serving actions. It was a perspective that served me well in the collective environment. I learned the hard way that it's a perspective that didn't bode well in an "Individualistic" society of born go-getters, an environment where the ability to communicate one's point of view precisely, eloquently, and convincingly is a virtue.

I discovered that the work place was another aspect of life in America where speaking up especially played a crucial rule. Americans are big on brain storming and strategizing about the next move to better improve their productivity or customer service. Weekly meetings are common and everyone in attendance is expected to contribute. My American colleagues, having been trained to always speak up in their best interest, are chomping at the bit, eager to have their input be heard. However, for someone like me who was not used to publically voicing my opinion, such settings can be unnerving.

In my early years in the American work force, I would always shy away from openly expressing my views. I feared that I might offend or show disrespect to anyone in the room who may not agree with me. I especially did not want to offend my superiors. Of course, I was bringing my "Collectivist" view to an "Individualistic" setting. My lack of input resulted in me coming across as having no opinion, or even worse, appearing uninterested with what was on the agenda.

In reality, it was only the cultural differences that kept me quiet. In fact, I had plenty to say, but was uncomfortable with the open forum setting. This was an important point I learned during my early days in the American corporate world, and one that had the potential to make or break my career. In my case, I eventually figured out what adjustments I had to make, but at a costly price of many missed opportunities.

Another potentially explosive topic in cultural differences is the meaning of the word "Yes." To straight-talking Americans, "Yes" really means yes, and they have no problem dealing with rejection that comes with the straight "No" as well. In contrast, Filipinos are strong believers in maintaining relationships at all costs. Consequently, in our attempt to keep the peace, the word "Yes" has morphed into multiple meanings. In **Kiss, Bow, Or Shake Hands**, Morrison & Conway wrote that in the Philippines "yes" can mean anything from, "I agree" to "maybe" to "I hope you can tell by my lack of enthusiasm that I really mean no."

When people are unfamiliar with this aspect of the Filipino culture, it can be frustrating, if not outright disappointing. I, too, was prone to saying "yes" to everything. I did not want to offend anyone with an outright "no," especially in the presence of others.

I recall an incident when I was in banking, and the head of H.R. department invited me to a company Christmas party at her house. She extended the invitation in the presence of several colleagues, so naturally I said yes as a way of being polite by not declining in front of the group. I never intended to go, so I didn't bother to show up to the party.

When this colleague saw me in the office after the Christmas break, she asked why I hadn't come to the party. I tried to wiggle my way out of it with more excuses, which she apparently did not buy. I finally confessed to her that it had been a cultural response to say yes to her invitation. She nearly blew her top as she reminded me, "Yes means yes, Ben! What kind of an excuse is that?"

My fruitless attempts to explain my culturally driven response only served to aggravate the situation.

Self-promotion is another topic that I once found inherently problematic due to my cultural upbringing. Americans see self-promotion as a natural way of serving their own best interest. Therefore, letting people know about their capabilities, goals, and achievements is perfectly acceptable. On the other hand, my Collectivist view collides fiercely with the American Individualist norms. This is what was happening to me in my earlier example, when I opted to take the humble route and downgraded my own performance evaluation, which consequently denied me the pay raise I was seeking.

How the world-renowned Filipino boxer Manny Pacquiao conducts himself in the public arena, offers another example of Filipino's negative view of self-promotion. During press conferences, Manny often shies away from bragging about his prowess in the ring. He also refuses to take cheap shots at his opponents outside of the ring. Unfortunately, his opponents often confuse his humbleness with weakness, get overconfident, and inevitably pay the price when they step into the ring with him.

By contrast, the popular television show **The Apprentice** provides a perfect example of the Individualistic view of self-promotion. In the boardroom scenes, Donald Trump often asks the candidates, "Why should I hire you?"

A common response to his question will sound something like, "Because I'm the greatest thing since the invention of the ironing board, Mr. Trump. You'd be a fool not to hire me."

In the United States, such an answer is perfectly acceptable. It projects the candidate's assertiveness, confidence, and take charge attitude. But in the Philippines, where humility and respect for authority are required, such boldness may not bode well for a candidate.

Over the years, I've gotten used to giving myself credit when it's due, to a point where I no longer feel the slightest hint of hesitation or guilt. Just the other day, I was asked if I knew how to Salsa dance. Shamelessly and without blinking an eye, I uttered, "In the world of Salsa dancing, I am a legend."

Indeed, I have assimilated to this part of the American culture very well - perhaps too well.

Addressing someone properly was another area that could easily be overlooked, but could potentially get things off to a rocky start, leaving a lasting negative impression on the offender's behalf. This is especially true when meeting someone for the first time. To Filipinos, respect for elders and those in roles of authority is a must and begins with how they are addressed. In a "Collective" culture, one can never refer to seniors by their first names. A title must be attached prior to their name: Mister, Uncle, Sir, etc. Addressing them by their first name is a sign of disrespect.

I also ran into the same dilemma in my early years in the United States, when my friends' parents often insisted on being called by their first name because addressing them "Mr." or "Mrs." made them feel old. It was a request that initially posed a huge problem for me, but now that I have adapted to the American culture, I have no qualms addressing elderly people by their first name.

Americans are not too hung up on titles. Even my American bosses don't see title such as "Sir" or Mr." as a necessity. Perhaps it has something to do with their individualistic makeup or outlook of self-preservation that ties Americans to their desire of remaining young at heart. Admittedly, these days, I do feel much older when someone addresses me as "Sir" or "Mr."

The issue of privacy is another topic worth mentioning. In an individualistic society, where independence and freedom of expression are heavily emphasized, privacy becomes an important necessity. Americans' desire for privacy is not readily understood in the Philippine culture. In contrast, Filipinos, with their group-oriented mindset, naturally prefer to surround themselves with as many companions as possible; the more, the merrier. For this reason, it is perfectly acceptable for relatives to live in the same household for an extended period of time. If the need to relocate arises, it's likely for family members to move in close proximity. Friends and family are always welcome to drop by; requiring them to get permission is considered insulting.

By contrast, Americans do not tolerate the invasion of their privacy by those dropping by unannounced. Family members are no exception; in some cases, it especially applies to them. I learned this lesson the hard way when my only friend flatly turned me away when I dropped in unannounced. It was a gesture that my friend obviously considered an invasion of his privacy. Americans, like everyone else, enjoy the presence of a good company, but it has to be agreed upon and not through undue pressure or obligation.

Americans embrace privacy as a positive thing. By contrast, Filipinos associate privacy with punishment. When Filipinos are offended, they hardly say anything about it. Instead, they would quietly walk away and manifest their displeasure by excommunicating the offender as a punishment. Whenever I saw someone being alone, I used to think that the person must have done something wrong to be rejected into isolation.

I was reminded of this during one of my visits to the Philippines. My relatives came by the hotel where I stayed, unannounced. After a couple of hours, my uncle suggested that since I travelled alone, some of them should stay to keep me company all day. I thoughtlessly requested for all of them to vacate the room, so I could have my privacy and get some rest. The room fell into silence, and my uncle looked dejected. I was jetlagged and preferred to have peace and quiet. I was only looking after my needs; a harmless gesture to an American, but devastating to my Filipino relatives.

Another major difference I've noticed between the American and Filipino cultures is the level of family involvement. Americans will only approach family members for help, especially financial help, as a last resort. They are likely to go to great extent to solve the problem on their own before going to family. The idea of being able to carry one's own weight holds a huge significance in the American psyche.

In the Filipino culture, family is likely to be the first option to solicit help from, particularly when it comes to financial matters. Family members see it as their responsibility to lend a helping hand and will go to great lengths to do so, even if it means self-sacrifice. It is not uncommon for Filipinos to come to the United States by themselves and send a substantial portion of what they earned to support family members back home.

I had an American friend who was married to a Filipina. He could not understand why she continually sent money to help relatives. To Filipinos, the obligation to extend financial help to family members is a lifetime commitment. Self-sacrifice for family members is an integral part of the Filipino culture.

On the other hand, the American side of me is skeptical about what can sometimes seem like a handout. This culture has taught me to be self-reliant and always look out for my own best interest. Helping others is a noble cause, but I have to be careful not to go overboard with my generosity to a point of creating dependency. I must also make sure that my good gestures do not put my finances in peril.

Cultural differences are evident even in the way Filipinos and Americans take care of their elders. Americans, often by choice, end up in nursing homes, while Filipinos typically live at home in the care of family members. My stepfather, an American, recently reminded the family that when he and my mother can no longer care for themselves, they would like to live in a nursing home. My sister expressed her interest in wanting to take care of my parents when the time comes, but Dad, true to his culture, has been adamant about not relying on any of his children.

The examples that I have cited are but a few, but I think they are sufficient to drive home the point that how we conduct ourselves (Cultural Norms) is irrevocably tied to our cultural foundation (Cultural Core).

The third and final layer of my fruit analogy is the part that is externally visible, the skin. It serves not only as the fruit's protective layer, it also coveys the message of what is on the inside. The skin allows us to identify and differentiate between a mango and an apple, for example. In a way, our gestures are similar to a fruit's outer layer, in that they are visible to the outside world and can give people the idea of who we are and what we're about. But unlike the fruit's readily identifiable and predictable properties, gestures are a bit more complicated because they don't always convey only one thing. For example, a harmless gesture in one culture may be viewed as completely inappropriate in another.

An example that comes to mind is the time I spent in Egypt during a sight-seeing tour in Cairo. Every time our Egyptian tour guide would announce our next destination, I would look him in the eye and flash the "okay" sign, forming a circle with my thumb and index finger. I often coupled my okay sign with a huge, cheesy smile.

I noticed that each time I made the gesture, the tour guide would squirm and roll his eyes before turning his head away from me. At the end of the day, the tour guide finally asked to have a word with me. He asked, "Why do you like to keep making those hand signals?"

I explained it was a gesture that meant I was in agreement with his suggestion.

He politely explained that in his country, the gesture had a totally different meaning. He said, "Here in Egypt, your 'okay' sign means that you are receptive to homosexual advances."

Shocked by what I heard, I pointed to his groin area and said, "Let me get this straight. The 'okay' sign means I want some of that?"

He said, "Yep! That's precisely what it means."

I quickly took a step back, paused momentarily, and we burst out laughing.

He added that there was another gesture I constantly did, that was also considered very offensive. He noted that throughout the day, I had been crossing my legs and pointing the sole of my feet directly at the person across from me. I told him that I meant no offense by it and only did it because it felt comfortable. He clarified that in that region of the world, pointing my foot at another man suggested that I considered him to be lower than the ground I walked on.

This experience reminds me of what happened to former President George W. Bush in 2008, when an Iraqi reporter hurled his shoe at him during a press-conference in Baghdad. To a casual American viewer, it probably seemed like as a silly act of defiance. But in the Middle East, such an act aimed at a powerful man, carried a huge symbolic significance.

To put these examples in context, imagine me conducting a business presentation to a potential client who happened to be of Middle Eastern descent. Whereby, at the conclusion of my presentation, I calmly take my seat across from him, carelessly crossing my legs with the sole of my foot pointing directly at him, and casually flashing the "okay" sign while asking, "So, do we have a deal, Mr. Customer?"

In this theoretical example, my seemingly innocent gestures have just greatly offended my client, and I have blown the prospective deal without even knowing it. This kind of encounter is not uncommon in major cities like Los Angeles, where a mosaic of cultural diversity exists. In such an environment, familiarity in cultural etiquette may be to one's advantage, personally and professionally. At the very least, one ought to know what cultural buttons not to push.

These were the challenges I encountered and the adjustments I had to make to assimilate to an entirely new culture. The development of the three components of my fruit analogy helped me manage the avalanche of conflicting information and allowed me to organize them into a comprehensive flow that made sense. The process enabled me to differentiate between my Collectivist Filipino upbringing and the Individualist underpinnings of the American mentality, thus allowing me to see the clear distinction and potential conflicts between them. Making sense of the cultural fog ultimately helped me clear the confusion I fell into along the way.

In my quest to learn more about cultural differences, I noticed two things about the published materials on the topic. Many are written like a textbook, with technical terms that could easily put someone like me to sleep. The rest of them are aimed at a corporate audience to show how to market products and services on a global scale. I couldn't find a book that depicted the impact of cultural differences from an immigrant's standpoint — the human side of the experience.

I wanted a perspective that provided a comprehensive look at an immigrant's plight: the life they knew, the ripple effect of the void felt by the family they've left behind, and a glimpse of the dizzying cultural divide that confronts them as they build a new life in a foreign land. I felt that this kind of multifaceted narrative was essential to fully grasp the power of culture. Since I couldn't find the book I was looking for, I decided to write it myself and have written it by way of storytelling – making it more interesting and easier to follow - with cultural differences as its underlying theme.

The following chapters chronicle my experience dealing with the inherent difficulties of assimilating to a new cultural terrain. It's a journey that begins in the Philippines, back to the humble roots of my initial cultural conditioning.

PART - II

MY INITIAL CULTURAL CONDITIONING:

THE UNFAMILIAR SIDE - A RANDOM WALK

CHAPTER 2

THE DICHOTOMY OF ABSOLUTE POVERTY: ALUMNOS AND THE GOLDEN FISH

"Make the most of yourself, for that is all there is of you."

– Doris M. Smith

***

The story of "The Golden Fish" was one of my favorite bedtime stories told by my grandmother. It was a tale about the little gold fish that could. The poor creature had the misfortune of living inside a toilet bowl. Each day posed a desperate battle for survival, as he was constantly subjected to the raging swirls of a flushing toilet. Despite his appalling pool of existence and the maddening dash to stay alive, somehow, flush after flush, the poor thing always managed to survive. His unbreakable will to stay alive enabled him to overcome however many flushes he had to endure each passing day.

Amazingly, in the face of his sad predicament, his optimism remained undeterred. He had triumphed over his miserable condition for so long that he started to believe that anything was possible. He convinced himself that if he worked and believed hard enough, he could turn his dorsal fins into a pair of wings - wings that could lift him up high above the confines of his limited existence and take him anywhere.

Day after day, he practiced flapping his dorsal fins as if they were a pair of wings. During the calm moments between each flush, he would vigorously flutter his frail little fins with seemingly no discernible difference, but the determined little creature never lost hope. He continued relentlessly, trying over and over again. Soon, he felt a slight improvement, making his efforts seem less and less difficult. He fluttered and fluttered endlessly until the day he found himself rising above the level of the toilet water. He could fly!

Every inch away from his revolting condition fueled his drive to flap his dorsal fins ever so swiftly. As he ascended high above the toilet bowl, an open window bursting with sunlight lured him across the room. Through the gleaming rays of the sun, he saw the most inviting sight imaginable: an open space.

With every ounce of his determination, the Little Fish That Could bolted out of his miserable existence and never looked back. He soared high above the mountains, valleys, and plains, zoomed through streams, rivers, and lakes. He flew and flew until he found refuge in a magnificent pond deep within the forest. And in the sanctuary of that cool, refreshing, crystal clear mountain water, the Golden Fish lived happily ever after.

Of all the many bedtime stories Grandma told, this particular story resonated with me deeply. In retrospect, I can see that it was because the people of the town where I spent most of my formative years shared the same misfortune as "The Golden Fish."

Alumnos is a small village by the sea, situated several miles west of Cebu City, Philippines. It was in late January 1968 that Grandma and I moved to this sleepy little town. In every sense of the word, life in Alumnos could only be described as absolute poverty. It's a place where hope is barely breathing, and for some, hope never had a chance. We lived in an environment where an entire day was spent towards finding the next meal. The concept of working to save money for a nice home, health insurance, college tuitions, or family vacations was a carrot on a stick that, for most, was a fantasy out of reach.

The Philippines, like most Third World countries, is a land of the "haves" and the "have-nots"; where one is either rich or poor. There is no middle class that is recognizable by Western standards. I happened to be born into the "have-nots" side. In my household, like most in my neighborhood, we could not afford to have such luxuries as running water, electricity, or a structurally sound shelter over our heads. We would get our water either from a well or by pumping it out of the ground, we used driftwood to cook our meals, and we slept on a hardwood floor. If someone suffered the misfortune of becoming seriously ill, they would simply die with no hope of medical attention.

But despite the difficulty of life in abject poverty, my fondest memories by far - which include the warmth of friendship and the feeling of belonging - transpired in that poor little village. In so many ways, the people of Alumnos made up for what the place lacked economically. They never spent their days complaining about their miserable conditions or feeling sorry for themselves. People just went about their daily struggle for survival while maintaining a great sense of humor and a prideful smile. Regardless of the hopelessness of their predicament, they aspired to better themselves with dignity, respect for the law, and devotion to their faith. I was in the company of people with similar resilience to that of "The Golden Fish," who were only trying to do the best they could with what little they had, in the circumstances they were born into.

In an environment where outside help such as government assistance was non-existent, the importance of family unity became even more crucial. People learned to help each other out, and neighbors become an extended part of the family. Crimes such as robbery, rape, and arson were never an issue in my days in Alumnos.

In my youth, my grandmother spared me from the hardships adults had to endure. My only responsibility was to keep myself occupied, and to that end, Alumnos was a paradise to me. I had the best of what nature had to offer as my playground: the pristine Pacific Ocean in my front yard, lush meadows in my back yard, an abundance of playmates, and all the time in the world to play and explore. Alumnos was a place where time was only a perception, not a master.

I can recall countless days spent on the beach, playing to our hearts' content. As the evening set in and our energies wound down, we'd sit on the shores in a circle and take turns telling stories. We let our imaginations run wild in an attempt to fulfill our curiosity and bewilderment of the world beyond our grasp. For example, one of us would cusp both hands filling it with sand and say to the group, "The grains of sand I scooped in my hands are probably more than the number of stars in the sky."

Another kid would chime in and innocently ask, "What are stars for?"

The genuine interaction with another human being was our main source of entertainment. In many ways, spending time together was far better than watching television. The adults in our community were masterful in the art of storytelling, and they had plenty of stories to tell. Among the children, the most popular topic of discussion was the fantasy of food. Every story started with different details, but in the end would always lead to a magical cave where wishes could come true. Most wishes involved a mile-long table full of food. We didn't know it, but we were fantasizing about a typical American buffet. Corned beef, fried chicken, and hot dogs were always popular on our fantasy menu. For those of us who never had enough to eat at home, these were luxury foods that could only be obtained in our wildest dreams.

About a mile across from shore, there was a small island that reminded me of a popular TV show at the time, "Gilligan's

Island." It was surrounded by colorful coral reefs and white sand that seemed to glow beneath the crystal clear water. The almond-shaped island had an old Spanish cannon mounted at its northern tip, pointed toward the nearby City of Cebu. Situated in the middle of the island was a white bungalow with a red tile roof, surrounded by palm trees and colorful wild flowers.

Kawit Island was rumored to have been owned by a doctor who lived in the city. Most Friday afternoons, a small yacht would dock on its small private pier, and a family would emerge from it. They would spend the weekend on the island until late Sunday afternoon, when they could be seen sailing back to the city. Access to the island was not restricted to the public, and the locals visited it frequently for family picnics, swimming, or simply to take afternoon naps.

At low tide, the water would recede so far out from the shores that we could almost walk to Kawit Island. People would descend from all around the neighboring villages to dig for clams or look for crustaceans trapped in the crevices of the coral reefs. In the evening, people would fish using lanterns that sparkled like fireflies across the horizon. Sometimes it seemed like there were more lanterns glowing on the ocean floor than there were stars in the sky.

Another treasure that made Alumnos a paradise to me was the enormous fish farm owned by the wealthy Del Rosario family. It was made up of several acres of land and divided into fifty ponds where Milkfish and Tilapias were bred. Every month, there was a harvest. Milkfish was an expensive delicacy and harvested down to the last fish. When it came to the inexpensive and less popular Tilapia, the farmers would allow the local kids to enter the pond and catch the leftovers.

My first experience wallowing in the muddy pond, chasing and catching live Tilapias with my bare hands, was incredible. It was so much fun that it became my obsession. Each morning before leaving for school, I would walk over to the Del Rosario property and peer over the cement walls to see if they were harvesting that day. If they were, I would skip school for the chance of being invited to catch the leftover fish. Every night, I'd pray for a Tilapia harvest to take place the following morning. On one occasion, I thought my prayers had been answered when I seemed to stumble upon a sure way of predicting the next Tilapia harvest.

It happened while I was daydreaming about catching those big, fat Tilapias in the middle of my fourth-grade class. My reverie was interrupted when my young teacher, whom I had a huge crush on, reached above the blackboard, raising the bottom of her skirt to such an extent that a portion of her underwear showed. I felt guilty for looking, but at the same time euphoric, as if I had just won the state lottery. The very next day, a Tilapia harvest was in progress. I thought, *wow, two lucky days in a row!*

A week or so later, the same thing happened. I was on my way to class and was about to climb the staircase when I looked up and saw my teacher at the top of the stairs. Suddenly, a gust of wind lifted her skirt before me. I caught another accidental glance of her underwear, and the next day, lo and behold, another Tilapia harvest followed.

By then, I was thoroughly convinced that there was a correlation between my teacher's underwear and the Tilapia harvest. I was so excited by my theory that I could not wait to tell it to my classmate and good friend, Edwin. Before class the next day, I made Edwin promise never to tell a soul of what I was about to tell him. After he agreed, I spilled the beans and told him everything. I must have been convincing, because Edwin was in complete agreement with my conclusion.

As I returned back to class after recess that day, all of my classmates were quiet as I entered the classroom. None of them were talking; they all just sat there and looked at me in a strange way. I asked what was going on, and a female classmate said, "Well did you catch many Tilapias today, you pervert?"

I could not believe that my good friend Edwin had thrown me under the bus and told the class about my lucky charm. That day was the beginning of the end of my passion for Tilapias. I prayed for days, that my teacher wouldn't hear a word about what had happened. Luckily for me, she never knew.

In my youth, films played an instrumental role in defining cultural norms and expectations. Every now and then, major brands such as Pepsi Cola and Tide would sponsor a public movie screening in front of the town's main chapel. It was a big deal, especially for children. Everyone in town would gather in the chapel's court yard to view the film. Movie viewing was a rare treat, for it provided temporary escape from the life we knew.

My movie heroes defined which behaviors were and were not acceptable. The common themes I found in Filipino films were: give generously, love unconditionally, and always forgive. Despite life in abject poverty, I can still recall bits and pieces of the way the people around me strived to live up to the ideals portrayed in cinemas. However, unlike the movies, in spite of the best intentions, real life stories don't always have happy endings.

My childhood memories in Alumnus were priceless. It was so much fun that, ironically, I even felt bad for the kids from well-to-do-families. From my point of view, they were like caged birds, living such a limited existence within the boundaries of their fancy homes. I would see these privileged children at their gates and inside their cars, as they came and went out of their fortresses. Other times, I would see them peering out of their bedroom windows on the upper floor, probably wondering what lay beyond the confines of their inborn prison cells.

I may have been poor, but I was free to roam the beaches, feel the freshness of the ocean breeze, run wildly through the open fields, and do it all in the company of my closest friends.

From a child's perspective, Alumnos was indeed a paradise. This is how I remember the place where I grew up.

In 1990, I returned to visit Alumnos for the first time after having been away for fifteen years. As an adult, seeing the economic realities of my town tainted the idealistic images I had treasured as a child. There were hardly any remnants of my town as I remembered it. The pristine beaches and cool turquoise water along the shores were all gone. All of its natural beauty had been replaced by modern progress in the form of landfills. Even Kawit Island has disappeared, buried beneath tons of gravel under a highway system that now runs through the reclaimed area that connected the City of Cebu to the far end of the Gulf.

A similar fate seemed to await my beloved fishponds as well. The vital sea water from the Pacific Ocean used to replenish the pond's water supply was no longer accessible. It's only a matter of time before they, too, would be buried underground. The families in my village, whose livelihood depended solely on the generosity of the open sea, were left to find other means of livelihood. They had no representation and received no apology or any form of compensation from the government or the private sector. Their source of income was simply taken away one day, and that was that.

By then, the population in Alumnos had quadrupled in size. I made my way through the maze of squalid flimsy homes made of weather-beaten plywood, woven bamboo strips, roofs from makeshift dried palm leaves, and patches of rusty, corrugated tin sheds. As I skipped and hopped over the crisscrossing veins of open raw sewage throughout acres of shanty homes, I didn't recognize any of the hardened faces that I came across. Life had taken its toll on the many faces I encountered, making them age far beyond their time.

Every now and then, I'd make eye contact with someone I recognized. One such encounter was with my friend Edwin, the kid who told on me and put an end to my Tilapia obsession. As our eyes met, he quickly lowered his gaze and avoided direct contact. Memories of our childhood came rushing through my mind; I stopped him and introduced myself. He paused for a second before a sign of recognition flashed in his eyes and a big smile lit up his face. Excited to see an old friend, I invited him for a bite to eat.

Initially, he showed reluctance to my offer, but I insisted and eventually persuaded him to agree. He was a bit uneasy in my presence at first, but after a few laughs, Edwin began to feel more at ease. He even brought up the Tilapia incident, and we had a good laugh. Our conversation then turned to the whereabouts of the friends we knew. I was delighted to hear that despite the harsh economic environment of our town, a few of our friends – like that of "The Golden Fish"- did manage to rise above the constricting walls of poverty.

One such kid was Genis Dumaguitte, my close childhood friend. The news that Genis did well for himself did not surprise me at all. Of all the friends I had, Genis was the person who had what it took to make it out. He was only one year older than me, but Genis was like a walking encyclopedia. I could approach him with any questions and he seemed to have all the answers.

I recall a time when, for some odd reason, I had acquired a curiosity about the banking industry. I found it odd that if customers deposited their money to the bank for safe keeping, then why would the bank be willing to pay interest to guard the depositors' money. In my mind, the customers should pay the bank for the service of keeping their money safe. I was extremely curious as to why and how could the bank afford to do so.

Genis explained to me that banks were not only for safekeeping, but also a place to make money grow. He then enlightened me with the concept of lending: how the depositors get a portion of the profits made by the banks from lending money to borrowers like homeowners and businesses. Genis was only eleven years old at the time.

After graduating college, Genis landed a job working for a German company and frequently traveled to Europe for work. He eventually married his college sweetheart and moved to another city, not far from Alumnos, where they raised a family.

The topic of conversation with Edwin then turned to my best friend in junior high school, Joselito Echivarria. Like me, Lito, as we called him, grew up in a single-parent household. Not surprisingly, I learned that Lito graduated from our class with honors and eventually went to college. He received a degree in Accounting and also became a Certified Public Accountant.

While working full time at a radio station, Lito would go to school in the evening to study engineering. He paid for the courses out of his own pocket. It took him years, but eventually Lito earned his engineering degree and found a lucrative career overseas. His family still resides in Alumnos while he presently works in Dubai.

It was so good to hear triumphant stories of friends who had persevered and succeeded. However, my conversation with Edwin also brought the sobering reality that for every success story in our neighborhood, there were many who had tried earnestly and had gotten nowhere. Many dropped out of school early on in favor of finding any manual labor jobs to help support their families. They took on work that barely paid enough to afford them decent meals or provide a sustainable living.

As the conversation with my childhood friend wound down, Edwin was apologetic for initially seeming unappreciative of my lunch invitation. He explained that he had been intimidated by my presence. As he put it, he saw me as someone way above him. His statement took me by surprise, and I asked why he felt that way. He went on to say, "Perhaps you were too young to remember when you were living here Ben, but in our society, there is an invisible line between the rich and us, the poor. I learned a long time ago to stay behind the line, where I belong."

I was touched by the sincerity of his answer, though I completely disagreed. But then again, as an adult, I had never been where he had been, fought the struggles he had endured, or experienced the consequences of living in abject poverty as he had. I was in no position to dismiss his opinion. For what it was worth, I tried to reassure him that I viewed him as a fellow human being and a friend.

At only 30 years old, Edwin already looked like a man soundly defeated by poverty's most crushing blow - the belief that he was not worthy of equality. Perhaps if I too had remained in such dire circumstances all my life, I might have shared the fate of so many of my friends. Fortunately, someone had always been looking out for me. My mother had the foresight and fortitude to leave everything behind and pave the way for me to have a brighter future in the United States. She made me a promise - a pledge - that she kept.

I was the lucky one.

CHAPTER 3

SACRIFICES AND CONSEQUENCES: LEFT BEHIND

"Life is a reflection of the voices we listen to."

-Patrick Bet-David

***

My earliest recollection of my mother is of me lying in bed beside her with my ear pressed against her stomach. My eyes were fixed on the flickering flame of a lantern across the room while I listened with bewilderment to the grumbling sounds in her stomach. I must have been four years old at the time. I asked her why she was making such a sound and how she could make it stop. My mother whispered gently, "Putting food in my tummy will make the sound go away."

Yolanda Sanchez is her name. She had smooth fair skin, which in Filipino society was highly admired. She also had a disarming smile that thinly veiled the hot temperament behind her sweet, innocent look. Her deceptively pleasant smile was probably the last thing that my father saw when he left for work on the day my mother ran away from him.

Years later, I learned the reason why she left my father, a man of whom I have no recollection. My only keepsakes of him are a couple of faded photographs from my baptism. In the pictures, Mom held me in her arms while my father stood proudly by her side. My mother was twenty years old when she had me, and my father was already in his late fifties. He was a movie distributor and well-connected to the local celebrities of his day. He was also a married man, with five children by his wife. My father maintained a couple of intimate relationships outside of his marriage, one of which was with my mother.

With the Catholic Church's powerful influence within the Filipino culture and government, divorce was restricted by law back in the day. Consequently, this practice led to the occurrence of married men, like my father, having mistresses on the side. Perhaps for his own convenience, my father housed both of his girlfriends in the same apartment complex in the city of Manila. Oddly enough, my mother and the other mistress became friends, and even creepier, my father impregnated both of them at around the same time.

When his wife learned of my mother's pregnancy, she discreetly offered Yolanda five hundred pesos to abort me. My mother laughed at the offer and told her to go away. Weeks later, my mother learned that his wife had extended the same offer to my father's other young mistress. The other woman had accepted the money and aborted the unborn child. In those days, abortions were crudely performed in dirty back rooms and unregulated clinics. It was in one of these places where the other young mistress had her procedure done and consequently bled to death.

The episode served as wake-up call for my mother. She realized that there was never going to be a future with my father, nor would he end his womanizing ways. It wasn't until months after I was born that my mother finally had the courage to pack a small suitcase and walked away from her three-year relationship with my father. We moved to the island of Cebu, where my mother was from. The year was 1961, I was six months old.

Three and half years later, there I was with Mom, listening to the funny grumbling sounds in her stomach. That same evening, I can also recall, her saying that soon we'd be moving to another place, a better place. Sure enough, not long after, we did just that. We rented one of the two bedrooms on the upper floor of a two story home in the city of Tres De Abril on Cebu Island. The second room in our unit was occupied by our housemate named Rosetta, who was also a single mother with a son. Mom worked long hours and I'd be stuck at home with Rosetta, who watched over me in Mom's absence.

Rosetta was a heavy set woman with a hearty laugh, who perspired a lot and was easily annoyed by my presence. I got along with her son Ray, who was a couple of years older than I was. I considered Ray to be my big brother and followed him everywhere he went, a move that nearly got me killed one afternoon.

The house we lived in was situated right along a bustling metropolitan street. One sunny afternoon, Ray and a group of kids had crossed the busy street to take a look at a dead bird on the ground. I wanted to see it too, but I was too small and slow to keep up with the rest of the kids. I managed to cross the street with the help of another kid who also lagged behind, but by the time I got there to see the dead bird, everyone had already crossed back to the other side of the street, including the kid who helped me.

I found myself alone on the wrong side of the street. I was scared and only wanted to be with the rest of the kids on the other side. Ray, along with the other kids, motioned and chanted for me to run across. I panicked and ran without looking at either side of the street. Suddenly I heard screaming, and then I felt something hit me. I stumbled and landed hard to the warm asphalt ground. The next thing I knew, I was looking straight up at an enormous belly of horse, with metal horse shoes thunderously crashing all around me.

I had been run over by an overloaded horse carriage that moved at a snail's pace. While still pinned underneath the wagon, I instinctively grabbed onto whatever I could and didn't let go. I was dragged for what seemed like miles before the driver realized what had happened and finally pulled the horse to a halt. Luckily, I walked away with only scraped knees and minor bruises. Mom and Rosetta got in a fight over the incident, and shortly thereafter, Mom and I moved again, to a house in the City of Mabolo.

Our new home was located in a nice, quiet, and safe neighborhood where I could play in front of the house without my mother worrying that I might be run over by a moving vehicle. It had two bedrooms, a decent sized living room, a big kitchen, and a spacious enclosed patio. An enormous tamarind tree stood guard at the main entrance. Best of all, my mother rented the entire house and brought our relatives to live with us.

It was in that wonderful home that I got to know my mother's side of the family. In all, there were six in our household: Grandma Rufina, Grandpa Antonio, and two of Mom's brothers - Uncle Segundo, her middle sibling, and Uncle Apolinario or Inar for short, her youngest brother. The only sibling who was missing was Mom's older brother, Anastacio, who lived in another town.

It was also during this time that I met to my sister, Gina. I don't remember Mom's pregnancy with my little sibling, nor do I recall ever meeting my half-sister's father. She was brought to our house one day and introduced to me as my baby sister. We were three years apart; I was five and she was about two. She lived with my mother's Aunt Domingga, or Mama Mingga, as Mom affectionately called her. Mama Mingga was the barren wife of my grandmother's brother who had died many years ago. She was a pleasant lady, well into her forties, with a warm personality and smiling eyes. I don't know the circumstances that led to the arrangement to have my sister reside with Mama Mingga, but I did know the close bond Mom had with her aunt.

Perhaps the arrangement was made so that Mama Mingga would not be so alone. Whatever the reason was, my little sister made Mama Mingga very happy. She was the apple of her eye. Mama Mingga often brought Gina over for weekend visits.

Life in Mabolo was grand, I was constantly in the company of family members, and never alone. At the time, Mother worked as a hostess at a nearby nightclub called Stardust. Her job required her to work evenings, and she didn't get home until dawn. She'd spend half of the day sleeping, but by noon, she always took me with her to run errands. Most afternoons, Grandma and Grandpa would take me to the playground behind the nearby cathedral. When neither of my grandparents was available, I can always count on one of my uncles to fill the void; they were always preoccupied doing something that piques my interest.

Uncle Inar, who was in his late teens, was a consummate prankster. He would tie a string in one of my mother's high heeled shoes and place it hanging just above the doorway out of plain sight. My uncle would hide in the corner of the room, holding the end of the string, and use me as a bait to lure unsuspecting victims to pass through the open door. When they complied, he would then abruptly release the string, allowing the shoe to drop on top of the victim's head. When the prank worked to perfection, Uncle Inar and I would roll on the floor laughing our heads off. But when Grandma became one of our victims, she promptly put an end to our source of amusement.

Uncle Segundo on the other hand, who was in his early twenties, was the disciplinarian of the family. He was a handsome, physically fit, no-nonsense type of man who believed that I was never too young to take things seriously. It was the side of him that annoyed me, but he also liked to do magic tricks for me. My favorite was when he made a quarter appear out of thin air and used the money to buy me a treat. I liked spending time with my uncles, and they seemed to always find time to be with me.

Mom even got me a dog, a black and white border collie named Snooky. I roamed the neighborhood with Snooky most days and spent a good part of my afternoons watching television with him. I loved watching cartoons, and "Popeye the Sailorman" was my favorite. We didn't own a TV set, but I knew the kids who did and befriended them all. With the help of my playful dog, whom the kids loved, I was insured a seat at show time.

There was one occasion when I may have gone a bit overboard in my effort to win over the approval of the kids with TV sets. Uncle Inar had made me an arrow out of a barbeque stick with four sawing needles securely fastened on its tip. Using a rubber band, he showed me how to shoot it in the air to hit a target. I couldn't wait to show off my new toy to my friends. In my attempt to really impress them, I convinced a little girl named Inject to volunteer as my target bearer. I had the poor girl lean back against the wall as I carefully placed a small fruit, the size of a cherry, on top of her head. I took my position about ten feet away, carefully aimed at the minuscule fruit, and fired.

I watched as the arrow twisted and turned, propelling almost in slow motion, toward the tiny fruit. Just when it was about to reach its target, its trajectory fizzled short and landed on her face. The poor girl stood there with an arrow dangling from her cheek. I freaked out when I saw it and ran straight home, screaming in fear.

I dashed home, only to discover that both of my grandparents were not there. From a distance, I heard my Uncle Segundo call out my name in a firm tone. Sensing that I was in deep trouble, I hid under the patio sofa. I saw my Uncle Segundo's feet as he entered the room, pacing back and forth as he continued to call out my name. I stayed hidden under the sofa for what seemed like infinity. Grandpa Antonio eventually arrived home and entered through the patio where I was hiding.

As soon as I saw him walk up the stairs in my direction, I bolted out from under the sofa and wrapped myself around his leg, begging for help. I confessed to Grandpa that I did not mean to kill my friend Inject. By then, Uncle Segundo was laughing, probably because he had been pacing for so long near my hiding spot without realizing I was there all along.

Grandpa Antonio took me back downstairs to see if the little girl was all right. Much to my surprise, Inject was more than okay. She was running around and playing as if nothing had ever happened. I was relieved to learn that her parents still welcomed me to watch cartoons at their house later that day.

Sunday afternoons were when I had the most fun, because that's when I get to spend time with my uncles. Mom would give me some money and one of my uncles would take me to the park, or the movies, or hangout with their cool friends. It was a treat that I always looked forward to. But there was one particular Sunday when neither of my uncles could take me out. Uncle Segundo's excuse was that he had a date with a girl, and so did Uncle Inar. Neither of them was available that day for the same reason, girls. Without a hint of hesitation, they took off in a hurry and just simply said to me, "Sorry kid - bye."

I was so disappointed, puzzled, and deflated that I just moped around the house that afternoon. Grandma Rufina noticed me languishing and asked why I wasn't outdoor playing. Instead of answering her question, I asked her why grown men were so preoccupied with chasing the opposite sex. My grandma smiled and answered my question the best way a child could understand; in the form of a story.

She began:

There once was a time when the gods and mortals lived in the same world. Together, they lived in perfect harmony; the gods going about their godly ways, and the mortals went about their mortal ways. It was a world of paradise for everyone.

But it all suddenly changed, the moment the mortals discovered all the wonders of being in love. The gods observed that when humans fall in love, they unite as one, and together they create a powerful synergy. The kind of power, they suspect, that could potentially rival to that of the gods, someday. This development made the gods very uncomfortable - a discomfort that quickly turned into paranoia as they discovered that more and more humans were falling in love. Ultimately, as their suspicions accelerated, the deities concluded it was too risky to have so many humans acquire the power of love; a risk they could not afford to take.

And so it was, the gods made the decision to remove all the mortals in love from their kingdom, and scattered them separately throughout the endless universe, to forever be apart.

Then Grandma paused briefly and said, "That is why, in this lifetime, you will instinctively spend the rest of your days searching for that special someone that was taken away from you. And that is what your Uncle Inar and Uncle Segundo are doing right this very minute: searching for their better halves."

My grandmother's story must have worked like a charm, because I was able to snapped out of my disappointment and happily went out to play with my dog the rest of the day. I eventually learned that my grandma's fascinating story came right out of Greek mythology. She had probably picked it up in her younger days when she worked as a nanny for wealthy families.

One sunny afternoon, a strange-looking man on a motorcycle appeared in front of our home. Like what my uncles had gone out to do, this man came to visit my mom in hopes of finding his better half. He wore a white polo shirt and black trousers, and had a very long nose. I was so fascinated by how different he looked that I stared at him constantly; marveling at his light brown hair, porcelain skin, and bright blue eyes. He was talking to my mom in our patio when he noticed me curiously peering by the door. He paused, turned my way, and said, "Hey kid! I'm Bill. What is your name?"

I had colors mixed up in English, so I thought "white" was "black" and vice versa. My immediate response was, "You're black."

He laughed and said, "No, I'm white."

I insisted, "You're black. I'm white."

Willard Long was his name, but my mom called him Bill. He was a serviceman in the United States Air Force stationed on the Island of Mactan, not far from our home. His movie star looks were reminiscent of popular celebrities of the day; Steve McQueen and Paul Newman combined. Bill was unassuming, a gentleman in every sense of the word, and he sincerely adored my mother. He quickly became a part of our family.

Bill would often take Mom and me for rides on his motorcycle; she rode behind him, with me in front, sitting on the gas tank and clinging giddily to the handle bars. We even had matching dark blue motorcycle jackets adorned with colorful emblems, with several zipper pockets. He would even take me onto the Air Force base to his barracks and introduce me to his friends. One of his soldier buddies gave me a really cool airplane model, complete with rotating propellers.

Bill genuinely liked having me around. We'd often go to a venue that had long electric tracks to run the colorful race car models he built for me. He would even accompany Mom to small villages to sponsor and participate in church related festivities known as Fiestas. The three of us would go on frequent outings to parks, beaches, ice-cream parlors, and baseball games. Bill really wanted to be a part of our lives, and within a brief period of time, this kindhearted American man filled the role of the father I never had.

He participated in a baseball league and would often take Mom and me to watch his team play. We were heading home after a game once, and rain started to pour on us. Bill pulled his motorcycle over to seek refuge at a tiny hole in the wall restaurant, where we ended up having a late lunch. An hour or so later, the rain finally stopped. We were about to head for the door when Bill took hold of my mom's hand and asked her to hold on for a second. He reached down into his pants pocket, pulled out a box and took the content out. Bill got down on one knee, presented a beautiful engagement ring to my mom, and asked her to marry him. My mom was teary-eyed as she accepted his proposal.

My mother and Bill wed on October 23, 1966. The wedding ceremony was held at a small chapel near the American Air Force base on Mactan Island. I was the ring bearer and got to stand behind the altar with Mom and Bill as they said their vows. Mom appeared stunningly beautiful in her wedding gown, and despite the tropical heat, Bill looked exceptionally handsome in his elegant two-piece suit.

The wedding reception followed soon after the ceremony, and was held at a fancy hotel restaurant in downtown Cebu. The celebration was attended by so many people, including distant relatives and Mom and Bill's circle of friends that I hadn't met before. I even got to meet the two girls that uncle Segundo and uncle Inar were so crazy about - the women they would eventually marry. It was a memorable occasion, full of cheers, like one big happy family.

A couple of months after the ceremony, Mom did her rounds of visits to friends and relatives. Her photographer friend followed us everywhere and snapped lots of pictures of Mom with everyone we visited. Little did I know, Mom was making these rounds because she was about to leave the country, and without me.

Bill's enlistment with the military was coming to an end, and soon he would be going back home to America with my mother. Grandma Rufina thought it may be a good idea for the young newlyweds to start on their own; settled down, get financially situated, and then send for my sister and me. It was a suggestion that made sense to my parents; they anticipated life in America was not going to be easy at the outset.

On the eve of their departure, I vaguely remember Mom waking me from a deep sleep. She had a bathrobe on that matched the white towel turban. Mom cried as she hugged and kissed me. "I will send for you - I promise," she said.

I didn't fully understand what was going on, and before falling back asleep, I sleepily replied, "Please bring me some nice toys tomorrow, Mommy."

When I awoke the following day, my parents were gone.

In the days that followed, the house became noticeably quieter. Prior to my mother's departure, both my uncles married and moved on; Uncle Inar had moved to another island, while Uncle Segundo moved to the countryside. The friends who used to regularly visited my mom and uncles didn't come around anymore. The only ones left were Grandma Rufina and Grandpa Antonio. Even my dog, Snooky, was no longer around. He followed me to the playground one day, where he was attacked by a dog with rabies. The disease later killed him.

Mom and I were inseparable before then, and I had never been apart from her for long periods of time. I was devastated and couldn't understand why she had to go, or whether or not she would come back. I thought I had done something bad to make her leave. I prayed and promised to be good forever if she would only come back to me.

Grandma Rufina tried to explain that my mother's absence was only temporary, but I was too young to understand; a moment of not seeing Mom seemed forever to me. I sat for hours each day and waited patiently at our patio window, looking for any signs of my mom's return. Sometimes, I would walk down to the street corner and watch every taxi that passed by, hoping that one of them would stop and bring Mom and Bill home.

For a while, I had a recurring dream of a passing yellow taxi cab with Mom seated in back seat. She looked straight at me as the taxi slowly rolled on by. I waved for her to stop the cab and let me in, but she just tilted her head down. I ran up next to her, banging my hand against the window, shouting for her to wait for me, but she just sat there motionless.

The driver sped away as I continued to chase after the speeding cab - lagging further and further behind as the dream faded gradually.

I'd wake up crying and panting every time, but Grandma Rufina was always there to calm me down, reassuring me that it was only a bad dream, and that Mom would be coming home soon.

My grandmother would often try to cheer me up by mimicking to thread a needle, just as she did the morning she found me setting alone looking out the window. It was an inside joke between us that started when she solicited my assistance to help her thread a needle. She loved to sew, but she often had trouble threading the needle on her own because of her poor eyesight.

Grandma comfortably sat me on her lap as she proceeded to teach me how to do the task properly. Holding a needle on one hand and a white strand on the other, she carefully aimed and slowly moved the thread towards the eye of the needle, but her unsteady hand kept the thread nowhere near its target. Grandma was blind as a bat and couldn't see that the thread was inches away from where she needed it to be. She poked the tread at the eye of the needle repeatedly, missing each time by a wide margin while saying, "See, this is how you properly do this."

It was the funniest thing I had ever seen. I asked her to repeat it again and again, with me laughing hysterically each time she did it. I laughed so hard my stomach hurt.

From then on, whenever Grandma wanted to cheer me up, she would simply mimic threading a needle, knowing that it would tickle me pink. This time though, not even Grandma's lighthearted attempt could cheer me up. Mom was gone and I didn't know if she was ever coming back.

My mother had done what millions of immigrants throughout the world must do to provide a better life for their families. Filipinos like any other expatriates, endure the hardships of an isolated life in a foreign land. They take on work as domestic helpers, janitors, and caretakers, thankless jobs that members of advanced societies frowned upon. Without protest, they quietly fulfill their obligations, abide by the rules of the host country, and look forward to the day when they can be, once again, reunited with their families.

Mom made sacrifices so that I could gain access to a brighter future but, consequently, it came at a stiff price of not having her much needed presence and guidance in my formative years. I was six years old when Mom migrated to the United States – many years rolled by, before I would see her again.

One month after her departure, my grandmother and I moved back to her home town of Alumnos, a small fishing village by the sea. To my confusion, Grandpa Antonio stayed behind, foreshadowing a family tragedy that I would soon uncover.

CHAPTER 4

LOVE UNCONDITIONALLY, GIVE GENEROUSLY, AND ALWAYS FORGIVE

"I've learned that people will forget what you said, people will forget what you did, but people will never forget how you made them feel."

-Maya Angelou

***

It has been said that extraordinary people are those who make the most of what little they have. If this statement holds true, then my grandmother reigned supreme when it came to being extraordinary.

Her name was Rufina Cabreros. As was common for her generation, she never acquired any formal education. She could neither read nor write, but she knew her environment well, had a solid work ethic, and always paid what she owed. The weight of our day-to-day survival rested solely on her frail and slender shoulders. Despite her shortcomings and the inadequacy of her economic environment, Grandma never complained, and she always managed to put food on the table. Her actions taught me the basic premise that nothing in life is free. Grandma Rufina was the person who had the least to give, but gave the most. She was my guardian, mentor, and hero.

Grandma was born during the great typhoon of 1912. Well, that was what she would always say to me whenever I asked about her birthday, which begs the question: How many typhoons were there in 1912, and which one was considered the "great" typhoon?

As a kid, I noticed that she, like many seniors of her generation, never celebrated her birthday. I realized later the reason why: they did not know their dates of birth. The Spaniards' colonization of the Philippines had ended only a few years before 1912, so birth record-keeping was not well established in much of the region. For this reason, my mother's side of the family tree only goes as far back as my grandmother. She often talked about our relatives and people she knew, but I was too young to appreciate the value of my ancestral history in the way that Grandma Rufina brought their stories to life.

For as long as I could recall, Grandma Rufina had always looked old to me. She gradually looked much older over the years as I grew under her care, but traces of her former beauty were undeniable. Her light skin, long nose, and high cheekbones set her apart from her siblings and peers. Grandma's once proud and squared shoulders were weighed down by years of life's hardships.

Her first husband, Santiago Sanchez, died during World War II. The circumstances surrounding my biological grandfather's death remain a mystery. They had five children, but only three survived: their oldest son, Anastacio, middle son, Segundo, and their youngest daughter, my mother Yolanda. Their two siblings, Marilyn and Victor, both died of pneumonia before they reached their teens. Grandma was later remarried to Grandpa Antonio Barrientos and together they had another child, my Uncle Inar.

As a provider, Grandma Rufina was tireless and never turned down any opportunities for work. Her primary source of income was selling seafood. She and her younger sister Francisca collaborated to earn their living - Francisca did the fishing, and Grandma sold the catch. Aunt Francisca, as I called her, would hit the shores before dawn and return with the day's catch by nine in the morning, catching mostly sea cucumbers and other slow-moving sea creatures.

It would typically take a couple of hours for my grandmother to clean and prepare the day's catch. By eleven, she would be on her way to make her sales route. She would neatly organize the selection of seafood on a circular bamboo tray and carry it on top of her head, freeing both arms to clutch a basket or two of extra goods to sell.

Under the blistering heat of a tropical sun, Grandma would spend the long afternoon making her sales route on foot in an area that spanned over ten miles. On a good day, she'd have everything sold by four o'clock and get back home at around five in the afternoon, completely exhausted.

When I was little, I would wait on our doorstep for her to return home. When I could finally spot her appearing at a distance, I would get so excited, like a puppy that hasn't seen its owner all day. I would run up to greet my grandmother, breathlessly jumping around her in circles. In retrospect, my little gesture probably brightened her day.

The day's earnings were divided equally between her and Aunt Francisca. Grandma's share typically averaged out to about five pesos – the equivalent of 75 cents in American dollars back in the late 1960's, or 12 cents by the 2015 conversion. With money in her pocket, she would buy ingredients for that evening's meal from the outdoor market. After supper, Grandma often hung out at a neighbor's house who had a transistor radio, and they listened to the evening news or drama programs. Finally, at around nine o'clock, she'd lay down to sleep in preparation for the whole cycle to start over again the following day.

It seems unfair for anyone to work so hard for such a meager return, but for my grandmother, days like the one described were actually the good days. There were certain times of the year, like during monsoon season, when the ocean was hostile and no fishing could be done. During these tough months, work was hard to come by. Grandma would take whatever work she could find, from babysitting, to doing laundry, to weaving palm leaves for roofing material. She took work that barely paid anything. There were times when she worked as a kitchen helper at a wedding or birthday party the entire day, just to bring home a plate of leftovers as payment at the end of the day.

No matter how long or hard Grandma worked under the table, she couldn't earn enough money to stash anything aside for savings. To compensate, she would collaborate with a neighbor on a unique kind of investment. The arrangement called for a partner, usually a friend or neighbor, to purchase a live piglet. Grandma's part was to adopt and nurture the animal until it produced a litter, which was then divided equally between the two partners. It was a long-term investment for both parties involved, and one that required mutual trust.

It was common practice to sell one's share of the litter before it was even born, which often involved discounting the price of the litter. The discount was done to entice other neighbors to buy, much like speculating on future options at the stock market. The practice of pre-selling the litter came in handy, especially when there was no work to be had. There were times, though, when Grandma ended up selling all her shares way before the piglets were born. The number of piglets sold in advance depended solely on Grandma's ability to make her potential buyer believe her prediction of how many piglets would be born.

On one occasion, Grandma forecasted that a particular pregnancy would yield around twenty piglets, and she sold all ten of her future shares. Her conclusion was not based on any scientific evidence, but rather on the size and shape of the hog's belly. As it turned out, the hog only gave birth to sixteen piglets.

Since grandma was only entitled to half of them, she ended up two piglets short of meeting her obligation.

The unwritten rule was that one must honor one's agreement. In this case, Grandma made up for her shortcoming during the next litter cycle and gave the buyers an extra piglet as interest. As impoverished as we all were, keeping one's word was still a valuable commodity in our community.

Grandma did what she had to do to put food on the table and I always respected her for it, but the one job she had that I completely disapproved of was when she worked as a maid for my classmate's family. I was thirteen years old at the time and was completely consumed with what my peers thought of me. I protested her taking the job because of what it might do to my reputation. I was afraid that my classmates would look down on me when they learned that my grandmother was my classmate's maid.

Pride, however, was not a luxury for the poor and hungry. Despite my pleading, Grandma had to take the job. My classmate's house just happened to be situated directly across from my school. From my classroom on the second floor, I could see my grandmother doing her chores diligently. She did laundry, gardening, cooking - anything to earn her keep. Watching her from a distance, working so hard and earnestly, I swallowed my pride and held my head high in support of Grandma's efforts.

Grandma actually seemed less stressed while working there, and she earned enough to cover our meals. I noticed that she even gained a little weight, an indication that the family she served treated her well by making sure that Grandma had enough to eat. However, her position would only last for a couple of months - their regular maid, who had been on emergency leave, came back and resumed her post. It was back to the drawing board for my grandmother. My classmate never did bring my grandma's job to anyone's attention; my silly fear never materialized.

Another incident when I thought my reputation was threatened by Grandma's presence happened on a late afternoon in front of my high school campus, Concord High. My entire class was on clean up duty along the main street outside of the school gate. We were spread along the side of the road, picking up trash and pulling weeds. As I squatted down, pulling weeds with my bare hands, I looked to my left, and much to my horror, saw my grandmother walking toward the school from just a short distance away.

She was on her way home after another long afternoon of selling her seafood in the sweltering heat. Grandma looked exhausted and unkempt. I was mortified by the thought that in minutes, she'd be parading her tired self in front of all my classmates, revealing just how desperately poor we were. She was advancing slowly toward us, and there was nothing I could do. I wanted to bury my face in the dirt.

I hunkered down with my head tilted toward the ground, my hands still anxiously pulling at the weeds in front of me. I waited for one of my classmates to identify my grandmother and begin the torment that would ruin my reputation forever. I braced myself for the inevitable. Any second now...

A minute passed, followed by another, and another, then nothing. I raised my head to look in both directions. Much to my surprise, Grandma was nowhere in sight. I breathed a sigh of relief.

Grandma Rufina was so attuned to my teenage idiosyncrasies that she had anticipated how embarrassed I would be if she were to appear disheveled around my classmates. To avoid being seen, she took a different - much longer - route to get home. I was relieved that she took the initiative not to embarrass me, but felt bad because I knew that she had walked an extra mile for me to save face.

When I got home from school that day, I gave her a big hug and thanked her. She asked what for, and we both pretended not to know the answer.

No matter how broke we were, once a year, Grandma always found a way to take me on a vacation. She liked to take me to Carmen, a farming community situated along the mountainside north of Cebu Island. All it cost us was bus fare and a small gift, usually a loaf of French bread, for the host family. We would stay with the family of a distant relative who lived on a small picturesque farm that sprawled along the foothills. I felt at one with nature there and looked forward to it year after year. But the most memorable childhood vacation I had with Grandma was when we travelled to the island of Negros to visit my Uncle Inar and his family.

The night before, I was brimming with excitement and could hardly contain myself on the prospect of seeing my favorite uncle once again. Grandma and I made our way to the bus terminal before the break of dawn. It was too early in the morning for regular buses to make their routes in our area, so we had to walk over a mile to the main street to catch a bus. Shortly after we started walking, we got picked up by a taxi driver who lived in our neighborhood, and drove us all the way to the main bus terminal for free.

We climbed aboard and sat in the back of what seemed to me like a gigantic bus. While we waited for the bus to get filled, Grandma got off for a moment and brought me back a rare treat: a glass of warm milk. It was one of those luxuries in life that we couldn't afford on a regular basis. I sat giddily in my window seat, sipping my glass of milk and eagerly anticipating the start of our journey. Suddenly, a boy in his late teens appeared next to me at the window and begged my grandmother for money. Grandma looked at him skeptically and replied, "Boy, aren't you ashamed of yourself, begging for money to a struggling old woman like me? You're a healthy young man, go find work and earn your money."

The boy stepped back and, without saying a word, he turned and walked away in embarrassment. At the time, I didn't understand what my grandmother was trying to teach him. I only felt sorry for the boy as I watched him disappear into the crowd with his head down.

As the morning sun began to raise, our bus finally rolled out of the main terminal, and I was elated. To reach our ferry at the far end of Cebu Island, the bus had to travel by way of the Manipis route; a one lane road that zigzagged between a rock wall and deep cliffs. As the bus maneuvered its way through the narrow road, I looked out the window and could barely see the ant-sized farmers tending the fields in the valley below. When we finally got past the nerve-wrecking Strait of Manipis, I was delighted to see a straight, flat surfaced street. We reached our destination just in time to board the ferry to the Island of Negros.

As we queued to board the ship, I couldn't help but notice that the wooden boat was barely floating. It was probably designed to accommodate a hundred people, but it looked like there were going to be around five hundred passengers that morning. The overloaded boat sat low on the ocean surface. Halfway through the two-hour ferry ride, there was no land in sight - only the sky and the deep blue sea.

I heard some passengers gasp as they pointed frantically to the left side of the boat. I stood up to look and saw looming dark figures a short distance from our ferry. It only took a moment for me to realize that they were blue whales. They looked so menacing in their natural habitat far away from the shoreline, and their massive backs seemed larger than the boat itself. At that point, I wasn't sure which was worse; the bus or the ferry ride.

As we sailed on, a school of dolphins raced along the side of our ferry. These amazing creatures performed acrobatic moves and seemed to enjoy showing off. As entertaining as these beautiful creatures were, I was glad when we finally docked.

Uncle Inar lived in a sleepy farming community a couple of hours' bus ride into the inland. During our month-long visit, we stayed with my uncle, his wife Nene, and their three-year old daughter. They lived in a small shanty hut on a hillside, surrounded by guava and mango trees.

The time I spent with Uncle Inar at the sugar cane plantation where he worked, is what I remember most about our vacation. He brought me to work one day to keep him company. My uncle had a designated area where he toiled from sunrise to sunset. He would cut the canes from their bases, strip the leaves from each one, bundle them, and load the harvest neatly into the back of a huge semi-truck.

Every few hours, a driver would take off with the full load, leaving behind another empty truck for my uncle to fill. The cycle of chopping, stripping, bundling, and loading repeated through the day. He worked alone without any help, under horrible working conditions.

In the field, he made sure I was always a few feet away from the sugar cane leaves that contained skin-irritating fibers. Uncle Inar told amazing stories and hilarious jokes all day long while he toiled. He spoke passionately about his plan of having his own farm someday. Uncle described in detail how he would put aside a portion of his earnings each payday until he could afford to buy a few live chicks and start a chicken farm. From poultry farming, he would expand his operations to include pigs and cattle.

Enthusiastically, he pointed to better days ahead, when he would be able to provide better accommodations for Grandma and me in our future visits. Judging by how hard my uncle worked and how determined he was about his future plans; I wholeheartedly believed every word he said.

At ten years old, I was too young to fully grasp just how little chance this man really had of ever freeing himself from the bondage of poverty. There was no system in place to protect someone like my uncle from exploitation. He was the product of an environment where the "golden rule" applied: those who have the gold make the rules.

He toiled at backbreaking work under inhumane conditions for seven pesos a day, which was the equivalent of one American dollar at the time. With his meager salary, he supported a family of three with another baby on the way. His employer offered him no benefits, not even a glass of water during work hours, but my uncle never complained or took anything for granted.

At the conclusion of our memorable vacation, I reflected on the exciting activities that I had done over the last month; picking wild fruits, fishing along the riverbanks, climbing hills and trees. But the most significant that stayed with me was the day I spent in the field with my uncle. I couldn't forget his enthusiasm and the earnestness pride he had in his work. He focused on what he had, and not on what he couldn't or didn't have. Uncle Inar was young, energetic, and full of hope for a bigger and brighter future. His inspirational work ethic was something to behold.

A couple of months after that brief but memorable look into my uncle's world, I received my first pay of twenty-one pesos. I earned it working after school at a souvenir shop, assembling coconut ashtrays carved into a shape of a monkey. It took me a month of work to take home what equated three American dollars.

I eagerly handed all my earnings to my grandmother and was surprised when she initially did not want to take the money.

She reasoned that I had earned it and should enjoy the fruit of my labor, but I insisted and eventually persuaded her to accept my earnings. Even then, she made sure that I kept enough to go see a movie and buy some snacks. For a couple of days, our meals were on me, allowing Grandma to have a short break. Being able to financially contribute for the first time was one of the proudest moments of my life.

Mom, while living in the United States, did her best to send money each month. However, she had her own family to support and could only send twenty, thirty, and on a rare occasion, fifty dollars per month. It just wasn't enough to support a family of three. Aside from Grandma and me, there was another mouth to feed, one whose appetite for more could never be satisfied.

It's a natural instinct for parents to want to spare their children from the economic hardships that they themselves have endured. I had the privilege of being able to enjoy my childhood because my grandmother did backbreaking work to provide me with that luxury. I understood that someday, I, too, would make the same sacrifice to provide those same privileges to my children.

Grandma's oldest son, Anastacio, witnessed her daily struggle for survival just as I did, but my uncle's take on it was completely different from mine. Somehow, Anastacio had taken Grandma's earnest efforts to mean that it was her lifelong responsibility to serve him. He truly believed that he was entitled to life's privileges without exerting any effort on his part.

I was six years old when Grandma and I moved to Alumnos after my mother's departure to America. It was then that I met uncle Anastacio, a slender man in his early thirties and the eldest of my three uncles. He lived with us, and by being the only male adult figure in my household, by default, he served as my male role model.

Unlike my hard-working Uncle Inar, Anastacio was the worst role model I could possibly have. Aside from his entitled mentality, he was also a violent drunk who'd spend every little bit of money he earned fishing on his alcohol addiction. He had an explosive temperament when drunk and was a true advocate of punishment; he would strike me with a closed fist, always aiming at my head. It didn't take long for me to get a taste of his wrath, and after a couple of these episodes, I learned to watch what I said and stay out of his way.

He came home drunk frequently, and my poor grandmother had to scramble to get me out of the house. She would drop me off at a neighbor's house for safety, while she went back and faced Anastacio's drunken rage. I remember being brought home by a neighbor in the morning of my uncle's first violent frenzies. As I entered the kitchen door, I saw Grandma tearfully hunched over the floor, trying to clear the broken things around her. After only one month of living with Anastacio, everything breakable that we had brought with us from our previous home had been shattered to bits and pieces.

It was a terrifying change coming from my mother's peaceful home in Mabolo to the destructive hands of this raging lunatic in Alumnos. There were times when Grandma could not get me out of the house fast enough, so we would weather the storm of my uncle's drunken fury together. Those times, I would just ball up in a corner of the room; hands over my ears, eyes closed, and pray that it would go away. In the middle of his rage, Anastacio would shout at the top of his lungs and destroy whatever he could lay his hands on. From a child's perspective, his crazed anger sounded like a lion's roar.

Perhaps the most painful scene for me to bear was how he would verbally cut Grandma to shreds in my presence. I never saw him strike my grandmother, but he would always curse at her and threaten physical violence. One time, he came towards Grandma and looked as though he was going to strike her. When I crossed his path attempting to stop him, my uncle picked up an empty bottle and struck me in the head with it. The bottle didn't break and I didn't bleed, but I did sustain a big lump on top of my head. I was around eight years old at the time.

Another incident that I will never forget is the time when Grandma couldn't find any work for the day. As a last resort, she took me to the beach and we spent most of the day digging for clams under the scorching sun. By late afternoon, we finally dug up enough clams to fill a small basket. Grandma then walked around the neighborhood, with me in tow, in search of a buyer. We eventually sold the clams and made just enough money to buy a cup of rice and a small mackerel for supper.

We hardly had anything to eat all day, and by the time dinner was finally served, I was starving and eager to indulge. Anastacio sat at the table and seemed annoyed. I thought he might be irritated because dinner was being served later than usual. When Grandma placed the clay pot of mackerel soup on the table, Anastacio took the ladle and scooped a little from the surface for a taste. He then made an exaggerated facial gesture to show his dislike of the food. Before Grandma could even take her place at the dinner table, Anastacio had already picked up the clay pot and smashed it against the wall. As he stormed out of the kitchen, he turned to my grandmother to say, "You make me sick, you old worthless bitch!"

I sat there, dumbfounded. The man didn't even consider what Grandma and I had gone through to earn that miniscule meal. We were fortunate that neither of us got burned by the hot soup thrown across the table. Grandma salvaged what she could from what had landed on the table, making sure that, at least, I had something to eat. However, after witnessing Anastacio's cruelty, I had lost my appetite. Neither of us had supper that evening.

The Filipino culture places tremendous significance on treating parents and the elderly with the utmost respect. I saw evidence of this behavior all around me, but unfortunately, the only rare exception just happened to exist in my household. I had never met or seen anyone who treated his mother as heartlessly as Anastacio did. I wanted to grow up in an instant just so I could pummel his face. Anastacio taught me how to hate, and I hated him with a passion.

Another family member who suffered under Anastacio's brutality was my step-grandfather Antonio. When we all lived in my mother's house in Mabolo, I never noticed any tension or animosity between Grandpa Antonio and my other Uncle Segundo. I can't recall a single incident in which the two of them had argued or fought over anything. They seemed to get along just fine. Little did I know that ten years earlier, Uncle Segundo and his older brother Anastacio had conspired to murder Grandpa Antonio.

The incident took place in 1950's, before I was even born. Uncle Segundo and Anastacio were still in their teens. Grandpa Antonio had the tendency to mouth off after several drinks and would get in arguments with Grandma Rufina. One particular argument must have gotten pretty heated, my uncles decided to take matters into their own hands, and hack their stepfather to pieces.

Segundo and Anastacio armed themselves with machetes and carried out the attack. Grandpa miraculously survived, but his right arm was mangled after using it to shield himself from the machete blows. The arm was saved, but it was deformed and paralyzed. Grandpa Antonio was a manual laborer, and losing the use of an arm was a virtual sentence of unemployment.

The boys were never prosecuted for their crime. Grandpa refused to press charges against the siblings, declaring that he had forgiven them for what they had done and that he was partly to blame. He did not see the need to ruin their young lives by sending them to prison. For this reason, Grandpa's own family never spoke to him again. They essentially disowned him for not wanting to punish my uncles.

Perhaps Grandpa did it out of love for my grandmother, or maybe he simply wanted to protect the boys from the danger of being incarcerated with hardened criminals. Either way, he stuck to his decision at the expense of losing the support of his side of the family. With no family to turn to, his life with Grandma was all that he really had. My grandparents knew of Anastacio's drinking problem and violent tendency, and Grandma thought it was best for Grandpa to remain in Mabolo when she and I moved to Alumnos.

Grandpa agreed to stay behind, but the separation away from Grandma proved to be unbearable for him. After six months, Grandpa decided to risk his life by moving to Alumnos to be with us. He probably thought that if he and Uncle Segundo could live in harmony like they had under my mom's roof, then the same could be done with Anastacio.

Anastacio, however, was nothing like Uncle Segundo; forgiveness and letting bygones be bygones were the furthest things from his mind. He was hell-bent on having nothing to do with Grandpa Antonio and warned the old man not to come near our home. A stern warning from Anastacio was enough to keep Grandpa from moving in with us. Handicapped, penniless, and with nowhere else to go, Grandpa Antonio became the only homeless man in Alumnos.

Grandpa held his ground and did not allow Anastacio's threats to drive him out of town. To get by, he took whatever work he could find. Grandpa Antonio slept in chapels, neighbors' patios, or in someone's boat, and despite his dire predicament, I never saw him beg for money. He was always protective of me and made me feel that he had my best interest at heart. There were times, when he would appear out of nowhere to ward off older kids who picked on me. Whenever I ran into him in the street, I would always hit him up for snacks.

Sometimes he would proudly reach into his pocket and come up with some change, and other times he would politely decline and say that he might have a little something for me next time.

When Anastacio wasn't home, Grandpa would quietly come by to help out around the house and have a bite to eat. He would lend a hand in cleaning and preparing the day's seafood catch for Grandma to sell. He would maneuver his way around the kitchen with Grandma and Aunt Francisca, until Anastacio would come home and drive the old man away. He knew better than to take Anastacio's threats lightly; Grandpa had received severe beatings from my uncle during a couple of their altercations.

One of these incidents happened on a late afternoon when I was nine years old. Grandpa Antonio felt compelled to share with me what he thought of my uncle; using the term "useless idiot."

I nodded in agreement as Grandpa carried on venting. We were having this talk outside my house; directly below Anastacio's bedroom window. Unbeknownst to us, my uncle was home, and had heard every word Grandpa said; turning it into a dangerous situation. Anastacio poked his head out of the window and angrily called out, "So you think I'm a useless idiot, huh?"

Defiantly, the old man stood his ground and replied, "Absolutely! I'm trying to keep my grandson from becoming like you."

With that said, Anastacio demanded that I get inside the house. My uncle huffed and puffed past me on his way to confront my frail, crippled, but stubborn grandfather. I feared for my grandpa's life and felt completely helpless in stopping whatever this beast was about to do to him. As soon as I stepped inside the house, I could already hear the old man moaning and groaning in pain from the beating. The awful sound of Anastacio's vicious repeated assault was more than I could stand. I stomped on the floor, bounced against the walls, and screamed as loudly as I could, "Stop it! Please stop!"

I continued to scream for help, hoping for anyone to intervene and stop the carnage, but no one came to help. The assault just went on and on. I placed my hands over my ears to muffle the ruckus, but there was no escaping that dreadful sound. I stormed out of the house and ran as fast as I could, far away from the terrible sound of Grandpa's beating.

I ran to the shore and kneeled on the beach, pounding the sand with my fists as I took all of my frustrations out. I went on and on and was still sobbing when I felt a hand over my shoulder, urging me to stop. I looked up and was astonished to see my grandfather standing over me. Sensing how distraught I must have been by what had happened, Grandpa came to find me to let me know he was okay. I was so happy to see him alive that I hugged and clung to him as tightly as I could. He assured me that everything was going to be alright and remained by my side until Grandma came home from work.

Two years after that dreadful incident, Uncle Segundo, his wife Benita, and their two boys relocated to Alumnos and temporarily moved-in with us at home. Anastacio kept the only bedroom we had to himself, while Uncle Segundo and his family occupied the small living room and Grandma and I slept in the kitchen.

Reuniting with Uncle Segundo and having him around the house was a welcomed change. His mere presence kept Anastacio's violent tendencies in check. Anastacio feared his younger brother. I learned that shortly after my uncles had tried to murder Grandpa Antonio, the two siblings had gotten into a deadly confrontation. The fight had stemmed from an argument Anastacio had with Uncle Segundo's best friend. Ironically, Uncle Segundo sided with his best friend and ended up nearly stabbing his older brother to death. He stabbed him seven times in the abdomen, but Anastacio, somehow, managed to survive.

It was also during Uncle Segundo's stay with us that he caught me, at age twelve, drinking beer at a neighbor's patio. He was livid and went on to lecture me in front of my friends about how good a job I did of following the path of an irresponsible drunk like Anastacio. It was embarrassing, but I understood that he was only doing what was culturally expected of him. Filipino relatives feel it's their responsibility to step-in with any family member they deemed to be heading in the wrong direction.

The phrase "Mind your own business" takes on a whole new meaning when applied to a culture that believes it is, in fact, their business to interfere. Telling my uncle to mind his own business would have been an utter sign of disrespect. I knew he meant well, so I listened attentively. Besides, when Uncle Segundo exerted himself physically or emotionally, he would get severe asthma attacks. I didn't want him to get worked up and trigger an attack, so I kept my calm as he scolded me.

After a yearlong stay with us, Uncle Segundo eventually moved his family to their own place just a couple of blocks away. Inevitably, Anastacio picked up where he had left off with his abusive behavior towards my grandmother and me. Grandma endured the abuse quietly and never sought protection from her other sons. She feared the worst of what might happen if Uncle Segundo retaliated with violence. Grandma Rufina would often remind me not to say anything to my uncle that it was a no-win situation; if one died, the other would surely go to prison. For this reason, Grandma and I had to resign ourselves to dealing with Anastacio's madness privately.

Despite our silence, word did eventually get back to Uncle Segundo about Anastacio's abusive treatment. As Grandma had predicted, Uncle Segundo retaliated with a vengeance. He planned to make his move at a time when he knew Grandma and I would be out of the house, around mid-afternoon. When the fight broke out, I was at the ashtray shop working part time after school.

Home was not too far away from the shop, and I could hear a collective scream from the crowd that was witnessing the battle between my uncles. The first thought that came to my mind was that a "cockfight" must have been going on, which often raised wild uproars from spectators. The ruckus got so loud prompting more curious onlookers to have a look. Then, one of my co-workers came running toward the assembly line to tell me that my uncles were involved in a scuffle. That's when my heart sank. I dropped everything and joined the herd of people running toward my home.

When I arrived, the fight was already over. Uncle Segundo was nowhere in sight, but I saw Anastacio sitting alone by our front door. His face was puffy and a chunk of flesh from his right bicep had been completely bitten off. He murmured something to me, but before I could make out what he was saying, onlookers were dispersing in fear. I took a few steps back to see at what was causing the neighbors to run, and that's when I saw Uncle Segundo marching toward us. This time, he was armed with a machete.

I turned to Anastacio and told him to run inside the house and lock the door. I had never seen Anastacio jump so quickly to obey anyone's command the way he did in that moment. Without saying a single word, he jumped to his feet, and rushed to hide inside.

I sat alone where Anastacio had been sitting just moments earlier. I didn't realize it then, but I was the only barrier that stood in front of the flimsy door between Uncle Segundo and Anastacio. I could have panicked and run with my neighbors, but somehow, I stayed. I sat there clasping my hands nervously at the thought that in the blink of an eye, this could all be over and one of my uncles would be dead.

Though my heart was filled with hatred for Anastacio, I did not want to see him die. Worse yet, what if Anastacio got the best of Uncle Segundo? What would happen to his family then? All of these thoughts were flashing through my mind when at the corner of my eye, Uncle Segundo appeared.

I could see the burning rage in his eyes. His gaze was stone cold, menacing, and unforgiving. Blinded by his fury, he hadn't noticed me until the very moment we came face to face at the door. He came to an abrupt halt, shook his head as if he had just woken from a trance, and without uttering a single word, he did an about face and walked away.

He could have easily pushed me aside and kicked the door open to ensure the conclusion of their battle. Fortunately, Uncle Segundo had enough sense to rise above his fury and spare me from witnessing the bloodshed. I was about twelve when it happened, and after that incident, Anastacio never laid a hand on me again.

After the grueling fight with his brother, Uncle Segundo suffered a severe asthma attack that lasted for days. That was his lot in life, recovering from one asthma attack to another. He spent countless days confined to his home. When he stayed with us, I could hear him heaving late at night, gasping for every breath. Since he could not afford to get proper treatment, his attacks would drag on for days, sometimes weeks. As he got older, they became more frequent and caused him to lose a significant amount of weight. It seemed like he was rarely in good health. On rare occasions when he was healthy, he would do manual labor, but it was always short-lived because of his asthma.

I remember when the owner of a dilapidated boat commissioned Uncle Segundo to hire a few men to deliver the vessel to a distant dock for repair. Uncle Segundo hired four other men, including Anastacio. Getting his brother involved with his project despite their differences was, perhaps, Uncle Segundo's attempt to reconcile their relationship.

It was good to see the two of them working together, as they discussed their strategy for the task at hand. However, when it came time to really make it happen, Anastacio fell short of expectations. Due to the lack of manpower and proper equipment, Anastacio concluded that their salvage project could never work and abruptly quit the job.

It took a while for Uncle Segundo and his remaining crew to get the job done, but much to everyone's surprise, they managed to deliver the boat on time. They devised a contraption made of empty barrels and ropes, which they placed firmly on each side of the boat to keep it afloat. The device held together well enough for the old boat to be towed away to its destination.

I was proud of my Uncle Segundo for accomplishing what Anastacio and other naysayers had thought was impossible. What was even more astonishing to me was the fact that Grandpa Antonio was one of the crew members Uncle Segundo had hired. He was still the crippled old man who never quit.

I can still recall the chat that led to Grandpa's hiring. It happened one evening when Grandpa and I were sitting on the beach watching the ships sail in and out of the distant harbor. Uncle Segundo happened to pass by and decided to join us. I thought it was a bit unusual, for I'd never really seen them talk to each other since our days together in Mabolo. The conversation started with a few pleasantries, but quickly turned on a serious note when Uncle Segundo brought up the incident of what he and his brother had done that nearly cost Grandpa Antonio his life.

Though the incident had happened many years ago, they had never said anything about it until then. Uncle Segundo was remorseful and tearfully apologized to the old man for what he had done. He was so distraught and overwhelmed with guilt that despite his tough guy persona, my uncle broke down like a child in our presence. I was only in my early teens, but even I felt the power and sincerity of his apology.

Grandpa said that he had never harbored any ill feelings towards the brothers for what happened, and took part of the blame himself. Sensing how distressed Uncle was, Grandpa leaned over, patted him on the back, and said, "I forgave you many years ago, you need to do the same."

The three of us stayed on the beach for another hour or so, reminiscing about the days we had in Mabolo with my mother. At the conclusion of our gathering, Uncle Segundo insisted that Grandpa join his small salvage crew. Grandpa accepted the offer; they shook hands and parted ways. It was a remarkable and an unexpected episode I treasured.

But the most memorable moment I had with the old man was the night I spent sleeping on cardboard boxes. I came home by myself, a day early ahead of Grandma during one of our annual vacations, when I crossed paths with Grandpa Antonio on the street. He was so happy to see me that I felt obliged to stay with him for a little while. We proceeded to our usual spot on the beach where I listened to him tell stories the entire afternoon.

Like most adults of his day, Grandpa was a natural storyteller. He spoke of life in Cebu during World War II, sharing his experience that though most Japanese soldiers he had encountered were militant, there were some who were not so bad. He described them as young men who were trapped in a role they had to carry out, even though they were just as vulnerable and scared as the rest of the populous.

He also spoke of his days working at a salt farm, where he saw Grandma Rufina for the first time; working side by side with Aunt Francisca. He looked forward to work each day, despite the harsh working conditions under the blistering sun, for a chance at seeing my grandmother. Excitedly, he recounted how he finally mustered the courage to approach her and say his first hello. I watched Grandpa's face light up with glee as he spoke fondly of the many trips they had taken together to neighboring islands, and how Grandma made him feel like the king of the world when Uncle Inar, his only son, was born.

Then at one point, he paused, pulled out his wallet, and carefully took out a faded photograph of the two of them together. They looked so young, happy, and in love; ready to take on the world. Grandma looked strikingly beautiful in her gray long skirt and white button-down blouse. Grandpa stood proudly next to her – with both arms healthy and strong - he looked like a complete man.

I enjoyed Grandpa's company so much that I ended up spending the night with him. We slept on cardboard boxes on the ledge of a wooden walkway by the shore outside a radio transmitter building. The spot we occupied had a great view of the city lights across the bay and the stars looming brilliantly above us. We didn't have blankets or pillows, but the magnificent view more than made up for the lack of amenities.

When I awoke at sunrise the following day, Grandpa was already up and gone. I gathered his cardboard boxes and neatly stacked them against the wall where he had them previously stored. As I was leaving, Grandpa reappeared to bring me a piece of a sugar-coated donut for breakfast. Delightedly, I broke it in half and handed him a piece. Grandpa declined and urged me to take the whole piece, insisting that he had already eaten his share. I was starving and readily took his word for it. In retrospect, I doubt if Grandpa could really afford to buy two donuts. Chances are he probably just wanted to make sure I had enough to eat.

In his own way, Grandpa Antonio did what he could to be with the woman he loved. Anywhere Grandma went, he would go too. He followed her despite the threats made on his life, the crippling assaults he received, and the homeless man he'd become. Grandpa held onto the remote hope that perhaps, one day, Anastacio would welcome him to our home. Mercilessly, my uncle never opened the door.

Love unconditionally, give unselfishly, and always forgive were the cultural norms that played out constantly in my day-to-day encounters with my community. These ideals reverberated everywhere: I hear them when I listened to Filipino songs and radio dramas, I saw traces of these themes in Filipino movies and stage plays that I had watched in my youth. And in many ways, the people of Alumnos have tried to live up to these principles. For some, the ideals paid off, but others, like my grandparents, were met with deadly consequences.

Grandma Rufina had the least to give but gave the most. Grandpa Antonio loved my grandmother unconditionally and faced the consequences unwaveringly. The two of them always forgave those who treated them unkindly. I will never know how someone like Uncle Anastacio could interpret good deeds as a free ticket to a lifelong entitlement. Perhaps it's just a part of the unpredictable nature of being human.

Initially, I thought that the people of Alumnos had tried to emulate these moral codes portrayed in Filipino music and movies, but the more I thought about it, the more I realized that I may have gotten it all backwards – perhaps, in actuality, the morsels of everyday life; defeats and victories, joy and sadness, and the never-ending battle of good versus evil are the substance of real life that various forms of arts have always tried to imitate.

CHAPTER 5

THE LOOMING CHANGE

"Time flies over us, but leaves its shadow behind."

- Nathaniel Hawthorne

***

I always used to hear elderly people ask, "Where did the time go?"

The idea of time slipping by so quickly baffled me because, from a child's perspective, time moved ever so slowly. Then, in an instant, my outlook of time changed when I received the unexpected news that my mother had followed through with her promise to send for me. She'd entrusted Aunt Prudencia, who lived in downtown Cebu City, to complete the immigration papers for my departure to the United States.

It should have been a call for a celebration because, after all, I was not relocating to just any other country; I was summoned to live in the United States of America, the most powerful country in the world. Everyone I knew was supportive of my chance to build a bright future in the land of opportunity.

Despite the accolades and positive assurances, I couldn't see past the idea of having to leave Grandma Rufina behind. To lose my grandmother in exchange for a better future was a trade I wasn't willing to make. The ground beneath me seemed to collapse the moment I learned the news of my imminent departure. I cried in secret every day over the thought that my time with Grandma Rufina would soon come to an end.

The date of my departure was looming, and now my perspective on time had taken on an entirely different meaning. My life had become an hour glass. Suddenly time was vital, and a day never seemed to be long enough. Every minute that ticked away was a tick closer to my dreaded day of departure. I felt like a death row inmate waiting anxiously for my sentence to be carried out. I equated leaving home with my own demise; dying to the things I had known, loved, and cherished. I wanted time to stand still and for the world to stop revolving, but time marched on with complete disregard for my desperate longing. My grandmother was everything to me - she was all I had.

At eight years old, I found myself asking, "Where did the time go?"

It's common knowledge that children are easily distracted, but in my case, distraction was no longer an option. With time quickly running out, I had to make each shred of every minute, hour, and day count. In my desperate attempt to avoid leaving home, I did not mince words, and I said the things I felt I needed to say. I went as far as making an overt threat to Grandma that I would kill myself if she ever let me go. It was a move that did not go so well with my grandmother, who scolded me for talking such nonsense.

In my next attempt, I wrote a letter to my mother and tried to build a case as to why I should remain in the Philippines. I tried to convince her that soon Grandma would be too old to take care of herself, that someone should be there looking out for her welfare, and that "someone", I argued, should be me. I also expressed my insecurities and fears of moving to America. I confessed that I felt I didn't belong in a world full of perfect people; that I was not smart or handsome enough to live there. I begged for my mother to just let me be.

With the exception of the neighbor who mailed the letter for me, no one knew about it until a reply arrived from Bill, my American stepfather. To everyone's surprise, the letter was addressed directly to me. Since neither of us spoke any English, Grandma Rufina had a neighbor do the translation. Filipinos lived in a close-knit community where neighbors are considered an extended part of the family, so, much to my horror, the translation was done in front of all of my curious neighbors.

In his letter, my stepfather complimented me for the courage it took to write such an honest and vulnerable letter. He assured me that I was a handsome and an intelligent boy worthy of being welcomed, not only in America, but anywhere in life.

Hearing those words back then did not mean much to me because it meant that I would still have to leave my home. My big secret was out and I was embarrassed, but the content of Bill's letter made my grandmother realize the seriousness of my desire to stay put. When everyone left the house, Grandma pulled me aside to talk about the letter.

She thanked me for wanting to take care of her in her golden years and acknowledged that she understood how much I wanted to remain at home. Grandma explained that her refusal for me to stay didn't mean that she no longer wanted me. In fact, the opposite was true. She assured me that someday, when I became a man, I would understand that she only had my best interest at heart.

I knew she meant well, but everything Grandma said just went in one ear and out the other. Unwilling to accept defeat, I saw our talk as my last opportunity to convince her to let me stay. I pleaded, "Why would you let me go? Why wouldn't you fight for me?"

Startled, Grandma said, "As I just told you, this is for your own good."

My eyes began to swell and I couldn't hold back the tears, "But Grandma, I never wanted to go. Please don't let me go."

Tears rolled down my grandmother's cheeks as she reasoned, "Any of the neighborhood kids would love to trade places with you. Why wouldn't you want to go? Can you tell me that?"

I tilted my head down to the floor trying to come up with something clever to say, but the only thing I could think of was the basic premise of how I truly felt. I told her, "I don't want to go because I can't stand the thought of me having plenty to eat, knowing you're back here starving to death."

Grandma placed her hand under my chin and gently tilted my head up for her to look me in the eyes. "You are a very thoughtful boy for thinking of me, but don't you worry about me. I know this is very hard for you to do, but just know that this is what I want for you, and trust that someday you will understand why I have to let you go."

Well, that was that. I knew then that leaving home was inevitable. I would have to accept my fate and try to enjoy what little time I had left. I tried so desperately to hold on to something I couldn't keep, the only thing that remained was the daunting task of coming to terms with what I was about to lose.

A few weeks after our final conversation about my leaving, Grandma helped me pack for my late afternoon departure. For my last meal, she prepared two fried eggs and a bowl of rice. Rice, a staple of the Filipino diet, was a luxury that many in my neighborhood could not afford. Instead, we would substitute rice with the much more affordable grated corn. It was just as filling, though not as coveted as rice. Having been served rice with fried eggs for my final meal was a treat. As I feasted, I remember thinking, *what a heavy price to pay for having such a great meal.*

After I finished my meal, Grandma and I took what was to be our last stroll at the beach. My aunt was already on her way to take me to the airport, and time was running out. We sat on a log and quietly watched the passing ships over the horizon. The momentary silence ended when my grandmother, in her soft voice, gave me her last words of advice: "Obey authority, do as you're told, work hard, and don't make any waves."

Her words were reflective of the life she knew. I nodded reluctantly in agreement. From a distance, we heard a woman's voice beckoning us to come ashore. It was one of my neighbors, undoubtedly with the news that my aunt had arrived. Grandma kissed me on the forehead and said the piercing words that I dreaded to hear: "The time has come."

I wrapped my little arms tightly around her waist as we slowly walked toward the lady who stood waiting for us. I kept my eyes fixed on the ground, not wanting to see us get closer and closer to what I considered to be the finish line; where the known ceased to exist and the unknown commenced.

When we finally reached my neighbor, the woman went on to say, "I have some bad news, kid. Your aunt sent a message that your trip has been postponed. She will send word of your new departure date in two weeks."

I had just been granted a reprieve, and though it was only for a little while longer, the news was music to my ears. My aunt turned out to be a heavy gambler and lost all the money meant to pay for my immigration costs. In fact, for years, she continued to milk my parents for what she could get out of them. I never expected my borrowed time to stretch out for years, but I never complained when it did. I considered each postponement a blessing because home is where I wanted to be.

As I transitioned into my early teens, my priorities began to shift. Teenage idiosyncrasies had taken over me. I suddenly cared about girls, being cool, and the need to appear tough. Peer pressure set in. All of a sudden, what my friends thought of me took center stage, and I became self-consciously aware of my economic status. Grandma detected the changes in my attitude and was gravely concerned.

The people in my community were law-abiding and God-fearing citizens, but there was a dark cloud looming overhead: the kids of my generation were coming of age. Grandma Rufina was too well aware of the troubles brewing in an environment that lacked the opportunities for higher learning and gainful employment.

Although rampant crimes such as robbery, rape, and drug dealing were never an issue in our community, random acts of violence were. This type of crime was mostly perpetrated by teenagers and usually had to do with alcohol consumptions or gang affiliations. My grandmother feared that within a few years, I could entangle myself into serious trouble.

What Grandma feared was not farfetched. At twelve years old, my friends and I were already idolizing a kid named Rudy; the leader of a small posse of trouble makers. Rudy was a stocky, handsome young man who had a touch of rhythmic swagger in his walk. He was respected amongst his peers, feared by his enemies, and adored by girls. It was through Rudy that I first witnessed a random act of violence in the street.

The tide was low that day, which brought kids from neighboring towns to frolic on the beach. I was on my way to school when I came across several kids scrambling to find a spot, on the side of the street, to discretely view a spectacle down the road that was about to unfold. I learned from one of them that Rudy and his gang were about to ambush a couple of unsuspecting kids from another town. I rushed to find a place, and managed to stick my head out just in time to witness the violence play out.

CULTURE CLASH

The two would-be victims were casually walking home, talking, laughing, and completely unaware of what was about to happen up ahead. They both had a fish in one hand and a fishing rod in the other.

Just up ahead, Rudy with his back against the wall of the corner store quietly waited. He held a sizable rock in one hand, eagerly anticipated for the boys to appear in his line of sight. Three other members of his posse positioned themselves on the other side of the street, ready to attack at Rudy's command.

As soon as the boys came within his range, Rudy ran up to them and punched the kid closest to him on the face. The poor guy staggered while his friend got beaten-up and dragged by the other members of Rudy's gang. After several seconds of frantic struggle, the victims managed to run away, dropping the fish and other belongings in the process. In a last-ditch effort to hurt them even more, Rudy hurled the rock he held in his hand, fortunately missing both boys.

I was really confused by what I had just witnessed. I didn't understand what the victims could have possibly done to deserve such a vicious attack. It was apparent to me that Rudy and his gang wasn't aiming to simply give those boys a scare; they were actually trying to maim them. The incident tainted the innocent view I had of gangs being a fun and friendly social medium to attract girls' attention. The image I had of Rudy as my personal hero was shattered, and the admiration I had for him turned to fear.

A month after that dreadful episode, I woke up to the news that Rudy and his posse had been gunned down the night before. Rudy was the only casualty after being struck twice; one bullet pierced his left arm and the other lodged in his abdomen. He made it to the hospital, where he was admitted for several days. Everybody thought Rudy was going pull through, but to everyone's surprise, he died a week later.

The news of Rudy's death sent shockwaves through our town. I, like so many of my friends, struggled to comprehend how a healthy young man like Rudy could die just like that. I was too naive to understand that death doesn't discriminate, believing it was reserved only for the sickly and the elderly. I couldn't wrap my mind around the idea of Rudy being dead. I had to see it to believe it.

It's customary for Filipino funerals to have the casket on display for public viewing for several days, sometimes weeks, or even a month. I viewed Rudy's remains in a wooden coffin that seemed too small for his wide frame. He looked stiff as a board, with not an ounce of life left in him. His eyes appeared to have been glued shut, and his face was covered with chalky orange makeup to camouflage the paleness of death. As the chorus of the mourners' cries reverberated all around the room, it was still hard for me to grasp that the lifeless body before me was that of the mighty Rudy. I walked away from the casket and headed for the door to catch my breath.

It's a curious thing how the memories we have of a person, whether few or many, suddenly come into sharp focus when we learn of their demise. As I stood away from the crowed of mourners, I thought of my first encounter with Rudy.

I was only six years old and had just recently moved to Alumnos. I met him during a San Juan Day, an annual occurrence when the ocean tide is higher and deeper than on any other day. Early that day, Grandma Rufina had warned me not to go near the water. She explained that many people, particularly children, had drowned during previous San Juan days. After hearing a few grisly examples from my grandmother, I obeyed her advice without resistance.

I really did intend to stay away from the water that day, I only changed my mind when I passed by the shore and saw my friend Rolly whose head was bobbing up and down in the deep end. I presumed that the water must not be that deep if Rolly, who was shorter than me, was able to touch the ground. It never occurred to me that my little friend was floating. Eager to play in the water, I decided to go in, but did not want Grandma finding out. So, I waited until all the beach goers had cleared the water.

At around 4 p.m. the coast was finally clear and everyone had gone home. I made my way atop a ten-foot tall coral wall that lined all around the Del Rosario property. The cemented wall separated the open sea from the fishponds behind it. I reached the far corner of the wall and carefully scanned the area, making sure that no one was around to witness what I was about to do. When I was absolutely certain that I was alone, I leaped into the deep ocean with delight.

The moment I plunged into the water, I knew instantly that I was in big trouble. The water was so deep that my feet didn't reach the ground. My eyes were wide open and burning from the salty water. I could only see a wall of green seawater, interrupted by the bubbles emanating from my frantic flail in an attempt to stay afloat. Up until then, I had only played at the shallow end of the beach and hadn't learned how to swim. Overwhelmed by sheer panic, the thought that rang loudly inside my head as I continued to sink deeper was, *Grandma was so right!*

Suddenly, someone jumped in the water and lifted me up to the surface. I heard a voice say, "Just take it easy, hold on to my shoulders, and I will take you to the shallow end."

I complied willingly, held on tightly, and didn't say a word. When we finally reached the shallow end, the rescuer said to me, "Didn't your mom ever tell you never to go in the water alone?"

The boy who saved my life that day was Rudy. He must have been around twelve years old at the time. If I had known that he was around, I would have waited until he was gone before jumping into the sea. Luckily, I didn't see him, and grateful for his quick instinct to save a drowning kid.

The memory faded and there he was, my hero, being laid to rest inside a cheap coffin; another victim of senseless violence. No matter how hard his loved ones prayed, begged, and cried for his resurrection, Rudy was gone and he was never coming back. He was only eighteen years old.

The flow of mourners continued to trickle in. I must have been in a trance as I timidly lurked on the patio, because I hadn't noticed that Grandma was in the crowd. Our eyes met and she made her way towards me. Grandma had a deep look of concern in her eyes. It was the sort of look that only a parent could fathom. She knew that in our environment, I could someday end up like Rudy.

Grandma was approaching and I feared she'd reprimand me for showing up at a funeral without her permission. Instead, she simply held out her hand and asked if I was ready to come home. I reached for her hand, she patted my shoulder, and we walked home.

Unfortunately, random acts of violence were not only confined to gang members, innocent bystanders were also impacted. The ill-fated incident that happened to Mr. Empe provides a case in point.

On a beautiful Sunday afternoon, Mr. Empe, a mild-mannered fisherman, left his house to move his small boat closer to shore before the tide got too high. On his way to the beach, he crossed paths with his next door neighbor who was carrying a fishing spear and was extremely drunk. No one knew exactly what transpired between the two men, but Mr. Empe ended up with a stab wound to his abdomen.

Word of the incident quickly spread throughout the neighborhood. When I arrived at the scene, Mr. Empe had already managed to make it back inside his home. Through his living room window, along with other nosey kids, I could see him crouching on the floor together with his wife who cradled him in her arms. The poor lady could only watch in horror as her husband continually screamed in agonizing pain. She tried desperately to reassure him that help was on the way. Minutes later, he fell silent. His wife shook the motionless body in her arms, and pleaded for him to come back – but Mr. Empe was gone.

His next door neighbor was arrested the following day. The man claimed to have no recollection of what he had done. As the authorities led him away, he cried and begged for forgiveness to the family whose lives he had destroyed. Mr. Empe was survived by his then-pregnant wife and two young children.

I came across another similar tragedy on my way home from school one afternoon. I was walking through a neighboring town that also had a fishpond farm, though much smaller than the one in Alumnos. A sizable group of onlookers had gathered on the side of the road gawking over something. As I drew near, more and more people joined the growing crowd.

I waded through the swarm of gatherers to satisfy my curiosity, and I noticed that everyone in the crowd just stood there silently. Lying on the ground was a dead boy about my age, twelve. He wore a pair of black shorts and a white t-shirt drenched in his own blood. A single bullet had entered through his left arm, a couple of inches below his shoulder, then pierced through his chest and exited on the other side of his ribcage.

The kid had been hanging around the fishpond, probably out of curiosity like my friends and I had done once or twice before. Rather than simply shout at the kid to go away, instead, the property owner picked up his rifle and shot him dead. As casually as disposing a bag of trash, he dragged the boy's body outside the property gate, leaving the corpse for everyone to see.

I kneeled down next to him and curiously looked over his remains. What I remember most about him were his eyes. They were wide open and completely dry. It seemed as though the moisture in his eyes drained along with the pool of blood that oozed out of his wounds. Dust particles had started to accumulate over his eyes, and they looked painfully dry. I thought of reaching over to close them with my hand, but I was too afraid to touch him.

It was almost midnight by the time word got around to the poor child's mother, who was beside herself when she came to claim the body. I never knew what happened to the land owner who shot the boy.

Violent deaths weren't the only danger we faced in Alumnos - there were also tragic accidents; mishaps that could have been easily prevented if common sense prevailed. Such was the case of another fisherman who lived on the other side of town.

While spear fishing at the deep end of the shore, the fisherman came upon a nest of live munitions scattered along the ocean floor, remnants from World War II. There were bombs and torpedoes still intact in their original casings. Under the cover of darkness, the fisherman and his friends sneaked a few bombs home and buried them under his house.

Then over drinks on a sunny afternoon, the fisherman and a couple of friends foolishly decided to cut open one of the bombs. The plan was to extract the powder and sell it on the black market. They proceeded with the extraction, using a hacksaw. It didn't take very long for the deadly consequences to occur - the bomb exploded - instantly killing everyone in the house.

I had skipped school that day and was at a Tilapia harvest at the fishpond farm. I was knee deep in the mud, clutching a live fish in my hands, when the massive boom shook the ground. I looked up and saw a small Cessna plane that had coincidentally flown near the explosion; I thought World War III had just begun.

Everyone in the pond, including me, rushed out to the safety of the solid ground. It only took a few minute for word to get out as to the exact location of the explosion. I washed up just enough to remove the mud on my hands and feet, and rushed to join the people heading towards the explosion site.

The fisherman's house sat on the edge of the shore, and directly behind his home was a full sized outdoor basketball court belonging to the town's main chapel that stood across the street from it. The roof of the house was completely blown off; all that remained standing of the two story structure was a couple of side walls. The fisherman's two youngest children, aged two and five, had been taking their afternoon nap upstairs when the bomb exploded. The blast shot them through the roof, like ragdolls; they crash landed next to each other on an open basketball court. Their torn bodies were covered with a yellow powdery substance, their little limbs mangled, and their skulls shattered. They lay in a pool of brain matter mixed with blood.

The scene was too gruesome for me to bear, and I felt nauseated. I ran to the nearest ditch, and just as I leaned over to vomit, I was faced with another corpse that was wedged in the muddy trench. It was him - the fisherman who had sawed into the bomb. The rancid smell of burnt flesh reeked from his remains. Both of his arms and legs were blown off, and he had a huge cavity in the middle of his chest. I could see the mud on the ground right through the gaping hole in his flesh.

I couldn't stomach seeing any more mangled corpses. All this time, Grandma had been frantically trying to find me. She was worried that I might have been one of the seven victims because of my tendency to roam around and being drawn to gathering crowds. I was in a daze and bore the expression of someone who had just seen a ghost when Grandma finally found me on the street corner. She was relieved to see that I was all right, though still a bit shaken.

I never learned the identities of the other four victims; I didn't want to know. I just wanted to distance myself from that horrific scene. The funerals for the victims were held at the main chapel, and I didn't dare go near it. Through the days that followed, I had recurring nightmares. I kept seeing those two mangled children, covered in that powdery yellow substance, crawling towards me and crying-out for help. It took several years for my community to get over this dreadful incident - but in due time, like everything else that came to pass, it was eventually forgotten.

Grandma knew all too well of the dangers and pitfalls inherent to our environment. She knew I could easily slip into a bad situation: hang out with the wrong crowd and land in jail or worse yet, end up dead. She understood that Alumnos may have been a tolerable place for a child, but for a young adult, the opportunity for trouble was all around. It was easy to see why Grandma was eager to send me off to my parents in America.

The person entrusted to handle my visa, Aunt Prudencia, continued to give my parents the run around. My aunt's household of six relied solely on her for support, and she didn't have steady employment. She kept her family and her gambling addiction afloat by constantly conning money out of my mom.

Gambling was viewed as a normal part of the Filipino culture. Almost everyone I knew gambled in one form or another; be it through cockfights, card games, Mahjong, or Jai Alai. Even the games children played had the elements of gambling in them - we gambled on games of rubber bands, marbles, Marvel cards, and even on live spider fights - there were always winners and losers, often employing the rule of "winner takes all."

Gambling activities were all around, and seeing my aunt spends days at the Mahjong table seemed normal. Year after year, she failed to complete my visa, and my parents continued to give in to her bogus excuses.

CULTURE CLASH

Through the years, departure dates came and went with the same predictable conclusion of cancelation after cancelation. I said my goodbyes to friends so many times that it had got to a point where no one believed I would ever leave.

On one occasion, Grandma and I even flew to Manila to catch my Pan-Am flight to Los Angeles. I, like everyone else, thought this trip was the real deal. But yet again, the plan fell through and I had to wait for another supposed departure date. Grandma flew home alone since we didn't have a return flight ticket for me. I had to travel back separately on a two day ferry ride back to Cebu. This particular failure to depart to America weighted heavily on me. I used the extra time to prepare myself for the inevitable ridicule from my friends.

The ferry finally docked at around noon upon its arrival in Cebu. I was too ashamed to go home and show my face in broad daylight. Instead, I roamed around the city and waited until late in the evening to sneak into town. The intrigue of my departure had been building up since I was eight, and now at fifteen, I was still stuck in Alumnos. My going away had become a big joke, and some of my friends started calling me "Joe," short for GI Joe, a nickname we used for Americans. I laughed it off, but deep inside, I was starting to like the idea of leaving home.

Increasingly, I had also become more aware of my economic status. I remember seeing photos in a magazine of rides and shows at Walt Disney's theme parks and thinking, *that can't be real*.

My mind could not fathom that such beauty could exist in the world, because such an awesome sight simply did not exist in my environment. My curiosity about the outside world began to flourish, an interest that propelled me to do some exploration of my own.

I never did well in school; classrooms bored me. I frequently skipped school and walked to the city, where I would spend my entire day sightseeing. During my eighth grade year, I spent more time exploring than I did in school.

For all its beauty and filth, I loved everything about downtown Cebu. I roamed the crowded streets, visited every cinema, climbed tall buildings, and window shopped at mega bazaar stores. I even wandered off to the main port of Cebu, where enormous cruise liners would come and go. I gazed at each departing ship with envy, fascinated by the vessel's capability to propel itself to faraway places all around the globe - a capacity that I, now, longed to have.

The ridicules and the reality of my economic status had gradually made me receptive to the idea of living abroad with my parents. It had been so long since I last saw my mother that the little memory I had of her was starting to fade away. My little sister, Gina, who hardly remembered anything about our mother, would always ask me to describe what recollection I had of Mom.

Though we lived in separate homes, Gina and I grew closer as we came of age. When we were little, I liked hanging around my little sister because she always had money to buy snacks. Her guardian, Mama Dominga, spoiled her to no end. There were times when I would hit Gina up for some change to play a song on a jukebox: I'd pretend I was going to play the songs she wanted, but once she dropped the coin in, I'd play my songs instead. I'd watch my little sister squirm in anger while I happily danced to my tunes.

I even sold jokes to my sister, charging her five cents each. I would always insist on collecting the payment upfront before telling her any. When I run out of jokes, I would resort to making up my own as I went along. Eventually, she would complain that my jokes weren't funny and demand her money back, but by then, we had already spent and eaten her change on snacks.

There was no limit to my scheming ways. On one occasion, Gina had asked me to accompany her downtown to buy postcards of Filipino heroes for a school project. We took the bus, and I helped her locate the postcards she wanted. Then I convinced my sister that if she hired me to sketch the twelve portraits she needed, her teacher would be so impressed with the amount of work she had put into the project that she'd get a better grade.

Gina eagerly agreed, but I still made her buy the postcards so I had something to copy from. For my service, I charged her 25 cents per portrait – naturally, cash in advance. I kept my end of the bargain and delivered the sketches on time. She later complained that my drawings had cost her more than the postcards did, and they didn't make one bit of a difference on her grade.

My sister's closeness to me and her tolerance for my behavior were probably due to the fact that I was her only direct tie to our mother. She loved to talk about Mom and would often ask me to repeat the same story of my time with our mother; how she looked, what kind of clothes she wore, what places we had been together. Gina always wanted to know if our mother was a good mom.

The problem was, as the years rolled by, the limited memories I had with Mom were steadily fading away. I even had trouble remembering what she looked like. I tried to hang on to what little memories I still had and described them as vividly as I could to my little sister - I knew it meant the world to her.

I longed to reunite with my mother, but the problem now was my Aunt Prudencia, who never seemed to run out of excuses in serving her own best interest. I had applauded her misdeeds when I wanted to stay, but now that I was ready and willing to leave, Aunt Prudencia became an obstacle.

Mom eventually caught on to my aunt's web of lies. For whatever reason, my mother had always idolized Aunt Prudencia. Perhaps the deceit lasted for as long as it did because of my mother's utmost loyalty and respect for her favorite cousin. I don't know the circumstances that prompted my mom's change of heart, but it must have been very difficult for her to finally accept that my aunt had betrayed her all along.

We received word from Mom that Aunt Prudencia was out of the picture, but she did not say who was going to take over or what I should expect from there on out. A couple of weeks went by, and I didn't hear a single word about my immigration status. The thought crossed my mind that, perhaps, Mom and Dad had given up on me. Maybe they had decided to cut their losses, since they had already lost so much money dealing with Aunt Prudencia. As the days continued to roll by without a word from Mom, the prospect of my departure steadily faded and my hope dimmed.

One month after Aunt Prudencia's dismissal, Mom made a call to one of our neighbors who had a telephone, letting us know that my stepfather was on his way to the Philippines to bring me back. I was elated to hear the news. An arrangement was made for Bill to stay at the home of a neighbor who was gracious enough to accommodate my stepfather's weeklong stay.

The following afternoon, from my window, I watched as my stepfather waddled through a crowed of children who flocked around him on the way to the house where he would be staying. It wasn't often that a poor town like Alumnos got a visit from a foreigner. The presence of my American stepfather created a buzz amongst my neighbors.

Half an hour later, I was summoned to come and meet him. I was only six years old the last time I had seen my stepfather. When I entered my neighbor's living room full of well-wishers and curious children, Bill was seated next to the host. He was sketching a map on a piece of paper while explaining to the man next to him, the sheer scale of the state of Texas.

From the corner of the room, I silently observed the man who would ultimately change the trajectory of my life. The last ten years had remarkably changed his physical appearance. He had gained some weight and lost most of his hair, but his baby blue eyes remained as radiant and kind as I remembered them.

When my presence in the room was brought to his attention, Bill stood up and approached me. At fifteen, I didn't think he would recognize me anymore. He looked at me intently, paused, and said to me, "I can see your mom's resemblance in you."

Then he hugged me. It was a hug that seemed to last long enough to make up for the years that my parents had been missing in my life. Bill, coming all the way to Alumnos to find me, had more than made up for the embarrassments I had endured over the years. He had gone out of his way to reunite me with my mother. His gesture reinforced the ingrained belief I had of the close ties Americans have with the Filipinos.

Ironically, on the eve of my departure, I chose not to have a farewell party. Instead, I opted to quietly spend the time with my teenage crush on her patio. Her name was Lillian; a kind girl with a radiant smile, who recently moved from another island. She asked how I felt about what lay ahead of me in America. I willingly shared the concerns I had of getting by in an environment where I don't speak the language. Empathetically, she acknowledged that it would be very difficult for me at first, but she also felt confident that, in due time, I would overcome it. I knew she meant well and appreciated her assurances, but deep inside, I was completely terrified.

My command of the English language was almost non-existent. Though I could read in English, I only understood a handful of words. I could not formulate a simple sentence, be it in writing or in conversation. Filipinos are known for their proficiency in English, but I had managed to be the exception. This problem was a direct consequence of my own making.

The Philippines is a fragmented country, geographically and linguistically. It consists of seven thousand, two hundred islands and has over one hundred different dialects. The dialects are so distinct that they are virtually different languages. For example, if a group of Filipinos from different islands get together and speak in their own dialects, they will not be able to understand each other.

When the Americans occupied the Philippines in the 1890s, after nearly four hundred years of Spanish colonization, they discovered that Spain had never established any means to educate the Filipino masses. There was no school system or form of government. The Americans recognized the challenges of the language barrier and deemed it necessary to have a universal language: English. As a result, all subjects in schools were taught in English, except for the subject called "Filipino" which was taught in Tagalog, a dialect spoken in the capital city of Manila.

I spoke neither English nor Tagalog, so I found it extremely difficult to comprehend what was being taught, as did most of the children in my class. School was an intimidating place, and many of my neighborhood friends dropped out of school at an early age. I grew to believe that my own dialect, Visayan, was not important because it wasn't recognized academically.

I used my lack of comprehension as an excuse not to take my studies seriously. I wish I could say that the language issue was the entire reason I opted to neglect my studies, but truth be told, I was just a lazy student who treated classrooms as my personal playground.

The years of neglecting my studies had resulted in my inability to speak the English language, and as I sat with Lillian on the eve of my departure, I realized that I was about to face the consequences of my ignorance.

On the morning of my departure, I was awakened by the chatter of neighbors who had gathered outside my home. It seemed as though everyone in town wanted to bid me farewell. They waited outside my home to shake my hand or pat me on the back and wish me luck. I spent the morning saying goodbye to each one of them before making my way to the house where Bill had been staying.

Our flight was scheduled to depart at noon, and by mid-morning, several taxi cabs were already on their way to take us to the airport. Shortly before it was time to go, Bill asked, "Aren't you going to say goodbye to your grandmother?"

With all the excitement that morning, I had completely forgotten about Grandma Rufina. Bill accompanied me as I walked over to the side of the house where I had last seen Grandma feeding her piglet that morning. I was surprised to find her in the same exact spot four hours later, still tending to her piglet. She was sitting on her heels, stooped to the ground with her back turned. I gently tapped her on the shoulder and announced that we were getting ready to leave, but Grandma did not budge. She kept her head down as she continued to stroke the piglet's back. I squatted next to her, thinking that maybe she hadn't heard me. Only then did I realize that Grandma had been crying all along.

The little boy in me, the one who was so attached to her, reemerged. Suddenly, I didn't want to leave her. I broke down and cried at the thought of leaving this frail old woman behind. I felt so badly for how callous I must have seemed when I'd virtually ignored her in my final days in Alumnos. But it was too late - my bags were packed, the taxis were waiting, and so much was at stake.

Bill helped my grandmother stand up as he tried to assure us both that everything was going to be alright. Grandma asked if I would be okay if she didn't walk me to the taxis to see me off. She explained that it would be a lot easier for her to stay behind and not to see me go. Reluctantly, I nodded and kissed her on the forehead goodbye. She handed me a handkerchief as she uttered her last word of advice to me, "Always be good."

Grandma sat back down and tended to her piglet as Bill and I made our way to the waiting taxis.

We had four taxi cabs to accommodate the family members and friends who wanted to accompany us to the airport. I sat in the very last vehicle of our little convoy with Uncle Segundo seated next to the driver and my sister Gina and I in the back seat. As we waited for everyone to load up, I reflected on how long it had taken for this day to finally arrive. I thought of the countless times I had said my goodbyes on that very same street corner, which was now filled with onlookers.

The convoy began to ascend, and I gazed at the faces in the crowd hoping for one last glimpse of the face I wanted most to see. As the taxi made its final turn at the corner, I turned around to look through the back window, still hoping for the remote chance of seeing her. Then suddenly, there she was, standing in the back of the crowd - Grandma Rufina appeared. . . She came to see me after all.

Our eyes met and my hand shook as I waved goodbye to her. She wiped the tears in her eyes, and the taxi sped away. Several children broke out from the crowd to chase the cabs, like my friends and I used to do. As we pulled further and further away, my eyes remained fixated on the street corner. I continued to stare until it faded from view.

PART — III

UNLEARNING MY DEEPLY HELD BELIEFS

CHAPTER 6

A STRANGE NEW WORLD

"The limits of my language means, the limits of my world."

– Ludwig Wittgenstein

***

Dad and I arrived at the Los Angeles International Airport at 8 p.m. on November 8, 1975. Our Pan-Am flight, which included short layovers in Guam and Honolulu, had taken over eighteen hours. My poor stepfather was in the plane with me all that time, mostly in silence as I wasn't saying much of anything. As we joined the long line of passengers inching to the exit of the plane, I nervously anticipated seeing my mother, whom I had not seen in almost ten years. I wondered if I'd be able to recognize her on my own. I could tell Dad was relieved once everything checked out at the Immigration Station and I was granted the green light to enter the United States.

As we walked through a throng of onlookers waiting at the arrival gate, I played a game in my head to see if I could spot my mother in the crowd. I scanned the line of faces as we made our way to the exit fairway. I then noticed a woman who shadowed us from behind the multitude of onlookers; she had long orange hair and wore a beige winter coat. She followed us excitedly towards the exit gate as she brushed tears from her eyes. I guessed that it had to be her, and indeed, it was.

Now in her mid-thirties, she was just as pretty as I had envisioned her to be. She wanted to see my teeth right away and was pleased to see that they looked healthy and straight. Mom explained that the last time she had seen me, all of my baby teeth were completely rotten. Her orange hair fascinated me, and I wondered all the while how it had turned such a florescent shade of orange.

We were then greeted by my parents' friends Millie and Ralph, who had accompanied Mom to the airport. My two siblings, both of whom I had never met, were also there to greet us - my half-sister Cathy was eight years old and my half-brother Glenn was five. They were so cute and cuddly that I kept squeezing their pudgy cheeks while we walked to the parking lot.

As soon as we stepped out of the airport, I was struck by the cool, crisp California air. It was unlike any cold temperature I had ever experienced outdoors. In contrast to the hot and humid climate that I was accustomed to, the brisk bite of November air made me feel as though the entire country was air-conditioned.

The seven of us sat comfortably in my parents' lime green Ford station wagon. Millie rode shotgun next to her husband Ralph, who did the driving, while Mom was seated between Dad and me in the backseat. My siblings curled up in a sleeping bag in the back end of the station wagon. My parents and their friends chatted as Ralph navigated out of the airport parking lot. I didn't understand a word they said, so Mom would sometimes lean into me to translate. I was content just sitting in my seat next to the window and enjoyed the ride. The full moon loomed spectacularly overhead, illuminating everything under its path.

Everything about my new environment was different, exciting, and strange. Even the one-hour drive home from the airport offered a world of new discoveries. My first experience being on the American freeway system was awe-inspiring. The freeway, as Mom had called it, was remarkably efficient, clean, and organized - multiple rows of cars smoothly glided along at a high rate of speed, unimpeded by traffic lights. Eerily, though, I didn't see a single pedestrian on either side of the massive roadway. It mystified me, because back home, I was so used to seeing thousands of pedestrians stampeding through the city streets at all hours.

I marveled at the spectacular skyscrapers as we passed through downtown Los Angeles. The tall buildings back home that impressed me was miniscule compared to these shimmering behemoths hovering over the metropolis. It was exactly how I imagined a mega-city should look.

Even the music playing on the radio was so different. It was energetic, vocal, and chaotic, unlike the sentimental melodic tunes I was accustomed to back home. I later learned the song I heard was "Rock n' Roll," by Led Zeppelin; a hard rock tune. I instantly liked the music because its energy level and excitement matched with what I felt inside.

As we drove further away from the city, we passed through several intertwining freeway overpasses, which reminded me of futuristic scenes I had seen in comic books. When we finally exited the freeway in the suburbs, I was riveted by the neat rows of beautiful homes, complete with manicured lawns and shiny automobiles parked in every driveway. We pulled into a driveway and it suddenly dawned on me that I have arrived. I was in America.

We lived in Fontana, California, a quiet suburb fifty miles east of Los Angeles. It was the home of a large steel mill, Kaiser Steel, where Dad worked as an overhead crane mechanic. Mom was a homemaker and devoted most of her time to caring for my two young siblings. Dad worked the night shift from eleven at night to seven in the morning. I hardly saw him during the week, but he would always reserve the weekends for the family.

We lived in a small, two-bedroom house on Valencia Avenue. The place may have been small, but compared to where I came from, it felt like I was living in a palace.

I arrived on a Thursday evening, and by the following Monday morning, my parents sent me off to school. Teenage years inherently, have their own set of challenges, but in my case, I had two additional major hurtles to deal with: the language barrier and the culture differences. At least the language barrier was obvious - I knew my shortcomings and what I needed to do to overcome them. The cultural differences were much harder to decipher. In fact, I was completely oblivious to their existence. My immediate concern when I started school was just to survive it.

I had always been a talkative kid; the quintessential motor mouth. But because I couldn't speak English, I had no choice but to remain silent. Not being able to communicate with anyone, with the exception of my mom, was a horrendous experience. I hated every minute of it.

I attended Saint Joseph Academy as an 8th grader, where I felt like an idiot every day. Each passing day was a terrifying ordeal. I couldn't make out what anyone was saying, and no one could understand me either. I couldn't utter a simple sentence on my own. I would have liked to be able to say, "I don't understand the words that are coming out of your mouth." Or better yet, "Please leave me alone until I'm forty."

I spent my time in class trying to figure out what was going on by intently observing the physical movements of my classmates. I mimicked them constantly to hide the fact that I was completely lost.

In a typical 45-minute lecture, I could maybe pick up a handful of words that I recognized, but I still had no clue of what the whole lecture was about or what I was supposed to do next. Usually, I would look for clues from my classmates. For example, if they collectively moved to look under their desks, I would know that we were supposed to take out a text book. But which book? I had to wait to see which text my classmates pulled out before I could do the same. I'd discretely glance at the student seated next to me to see what page he was on, and then turn to it as well.

I repeated this nightmarish cycle of observing, guessing, and mimicking throughout all of my classes. I'd pull myself together each night and muster all the courage I had to once again face the following day's uncertainties. It was a nerve-wrecking experience that manifested itself in recurring dreams I had of being buried alive under an avalanche of printed words.

In the dream, I'd be sitting in a room somewhere and the ceiling would start raining printed words: the size of the words in textbooks. It would start as a trickle, and then pour hard. I'd end-up getting buried under a mountain of these words and claw my way to the top. Sometimes I'd make it to the surface and other times not, but either way, I always woke up gasping for air. Perhaps subconsciously, I was anxious about the tons of words I still needed to learn.

During my second week of school, my Social Studies teacher to whom my classmates fondly referred as "Sister Mary Elephant," assigned for me to do a class presentation. She wanted me to play a song in class, share my interpretation of what the song was about, and conclude with a question and answer session with my classmates.

I knew immediately that it was way in over my head, but didn't object while in class. However, during lunch break, I gathered all the English words I could put together and approached my teacher. I meant to tell her that I was not ready to take on such a complicated project. In actuality, I think I uttered something like, "I, no can do. Please."

I must have gotten my point across, because she looked at me with disgust as she peered over her black-rimmed eyeglasses and asked, "Why should you be so special?"

I understood her objection clearly and felt embarrassed for even asking for an exemption, but the project was far more than I could handle. My English was so bad that I couldn't even provide a reason as to why I should be excused from the project. I could only shrug my shoulders in defeat as I watched her turn and walk away.

I had never imagined that a nun could be so mean. Right then and there, I understood why my classmates liked to make fun of her behind her back. When the day came for me to do my presentation, I remained seated and just shrugged my shoulders in defiance, each time she repeatedly called out my name. After her relentless, but unsuccessful attempt to get me to perform, she finally had enough, cut her losses, and moved on to the next student.

As if my ordeal wasn't difficult enough, one month after I started school, I found myself involuntarily appointed to join the school's basketball team. I wanted no part of it, but Saint Joe was such a small school that the seventh and eighth graders combined had barely enough boys to form a team. Needless to say, they needed all the able-bodies available to participate. By default, I had to be a part of Saint Joe's 1976 basketball team. It was another addition to my nightmarish circumstance, but I did manage to play the whole season, and even made a couple of memorable plays.

Though I had some good times being on the team, in my situation, embarrassing moments were inevitable. I recall an incident one afternoon that, even now, can still make my skin crawl. During practice, my young coach Richard Romeo kept screaming at me to, "Switch, Ben! Switch!"

I tried to ignore him, but he kept calling for me to switch. Up until then, the only meaning of the word "switch" I knew of was that of a light switch. I thought he was yelling for me to turn off the lights, which I found very strange. If that was the case, why couldn't he do it himself? Obviously, I was busy practicing. But the more I ignored my coach, the louder he got. Reluctantly, I got off the basketball court and headed towards the far end of the gym to find the light switch. By then, my coach was practically pulling his hair out in frustration, "Ben! Ben! Where are you going?"

Little did I know that what he was trying to tell me all along was for me to switch my position on the court. I had no idea that "switch" also meant "trade places." Baffled by my actions, Coach Romeo and my teammates annoyingly threw their hands up in the air.

In the back of my mind, I thought, *Yeah, welcome to my world, bitches!*

Another embarrassing episode followed almost immediately. I was on my way out the door, when my coach pulled me aside to remind me about our first playoff game the next day. I nodded excitedly and went on my way. I took the word "playoff" to mean that we did not have a game. It sounded like a short way of saying "the play is off."

In my confusion, I didn't bother to show up for the important game the following day. When I saw Coach Romeo again, he was very disappointed that I had not gone to the critical playoff game. He said that we had only lost by three points, and my presence would have made a world of difference. I was too embarrassed to explain the reason why I was a no-show. At the conclusion of the basketball season, Saint Joseph came in third place. We could have probably done much better if I had only known what "playoff" meant.

My day-to-day existence outside of school was mundane and utterly uneventful. I stayed home a lot, but didn't mind it so much since I couldn't communicate with the outside world anyway. At home, I felt safe and shielded. My life in America was a reversal of the life I knew before: I now had plenty to eat, but socially, I was starving.

One of my observations about Americans was that they live in seclusion and seem to treasure their privacy. They also rarely ventured outside of their homes. I remember visiting my only friend from school, Matt Smerber. I hadn't told him I was coming, so he was very surprised and seemingly irritated when he saw me at his front door. Matt advised me to always call first and not just drop by like I had. He then turned around and shut the door. I walked away devastated and shocked; wondering what I had done to deserve such blatant rejection.

At that point, my parents had lived on Valencia Avenue for a decade and, yet, they only knew a couple of families in our block. Our street was always eerily quiet and undisturbed. I could always tell when a neighbor had company over or was throwing a party, based on the extra cars parked in their driveways. These occasions were very seldom. The American obsession with privacy was puzzling to me.

The way the Americans behaved struck me as being incredibly selfish. They seemed to only care about themselves, and showed little regard to authority figures. I heard young people address their elders by their first names. This type of insubordination was never tolerated in the Philippines. I ran into this dilemma when my friend Matt first introduced me to his father, who firmly shook my hand and insisted, "Ben, you make me feel old when you call me Mr. Smerber. Please call me Jim."

His request posed a huge problem for me because he was obviously older than I was, and there was no way I could get myself to call him by his first name. I felt that it was just too disrespectful, but at the same time, I did not want to offend him by using the title "Mr."

As a compromise to myself, I simply avoided him as much as I possibly could. When I couldn't, I would just mumble his name.

I could live with the mumbling, but never the outright pronunciation of, "Jim."

Another American custom I was appalled by was when my classmates would eat in front of me and not offer to share their food. Where I'm from, even if we didn't have enough on our plate for ourselves, it was a customarily polite gesture to offer to share a meal with company. It showed consideration for others.

I didn't understand it at the time that my views were the reflections of my Filipino conditioning, and likewise, the behaviors I encountered with my friends were only cultural expressions of how Americans are supposed to act. My lack of understanding to these cultural differences, lead me to take offense at behaviors that were at odds with mine. My day-to-day affairs turned into a guessing game of what strange or offensive behavior I would encounter that day.

One year after I joined the family in America, my stepfather legally adopted me as his son. Just as he has since the day we met, Dad had always treated me as his own. Anywhere we went, he would always introduce me to everyone he knew as his son. The man was a gift - he had always been the father I never had. I was as proud then, as I am today, to carry his family name.

In that same year, we moved to a much larger house on Tangelo Avenue, not far from the location of our old home. The house was brand new with three bedrooms, two spacious living rooms, a fireplace, two bathrooms, a nice kitchen, and sizable front and back yards. We spent most of that summer working on the yards - we removed tons of gravel and rocks from the soil, laid down the sprinkler system, and planted grass, shrubs, and trees.

My parents occupied the master bedroom, Cathy and Glenn shared the second largest bedroom, and I had a bedroom all to myself, something I never had before. I had shared the small sleeping quarters with my grandmother the entire time I was in the Philippines. It felt very strange to suddenly have what seemed like an excessive amount of space and privacy. The physical isolation of having my own room, felt more like a punishment than a reward.

At that stage, I was old enough to help out with babysitting my siblings. Mom took this opportunity to find work to help pay the mortgage and start saving to bring my sister Gina over from the Philippines. She found a job as a cashier at a gas station on Cherry Ave, right off the freeway. Like Dad, she also worked the graveyard shift. With both of them working night shifts and sleeping during the day, I really didn't have much adult supervision. I mostly did as I pleased and developed a bad habit of staying awake all night watching television.

Ironically, the countless hours I spent in front of the television actually helped improve my English. One of the challenges I had with the English language was the sheer speed of the spoken language. Americans speak too fast and I simply could not keep up with the pace, which to me sounded like blurred words. Watching television helped my ears get used to the tempo and tone of the spoken words, to a point where I could pick up what was being said. It was one of those rare exceptions when I could claim the countless hours I spent in front of the television as productive use of time. Inevitably, my late-night habit had its consequences. I suffered from lack of sleep, especially during the school week. I felt sluggish throughout the day and wasn't always at my best.

My parents were not at all the disciplinarian types. In fact, the two of them were very laid back. They never imposed a set of rules or assigned any responsibilities for me to follow. I just took the initiative and quietly did what I could do to help; chores around the house and tried not to bring any problems home.

I transferred to a public school for my remaining time in junior and high school. I went through the motions of going to school, but old habits are hard to break. The lack of discipline I had developed in the Philippines unabatedly remained. As always has been the case, school settings bored me. With the bad sleeping patterns that I had developed, along with the language barrier, and lack of parental supervision, I started cutting classes again in the tenth grade. The big difference this time was that I didn't have anywhere exciting to go. There wasn't much to see in the small town of Fontana. Instead of looking conspicuous walking alone in suburban streets with hardly any other pedestrian in it, I developed a new routine.

I'd set my alarm clock for 6:45 a.m., just before my parents came home from work, and I would watch TV until 4 a.m. I would drag myself out of bed and marched right into my walk-in closet where I would sleep until 2 p.m. Then climb out my bedroom window, go around to the front door and ring the doorbell, pretending as if I was coming home from school.

This went on for a while, until Dad caught me sleeping in the closet. I had dreamt one morning that my dad walked in my room, opened my closet doors, and found me snoring in my sleep. He asked, "What are you doing home, Benjie?" as I woke up from the dream.

Coincidentally, the very next day, the exact situation happened just the way I had dreamt it. I couldn't believe it was happening. Dad repeated his question, "I said, what are you doing home, son?"

Awkwardly I replied, "I missed my bus, Dad."

Without a hint of anger, he calmly said, "Let's go, son. I'll take you to school. Hurry, before your mother sees you."

I was devastated for disappointing Dad, and from that point on, I made a concerted effort to attend all my classes even though I hated school.

Two years had gone by since my arrival, and my English still hadn't improved much at all. The nightmarish scenario I encountered in classrooms still remained. Being put on the spot in front of my class to answer questions I didn't understand was the worst part. In my Political Science class, our teacher once posed the question, "Will a woman ever be elected President of the United States?"

He scanned the classroom for someone to provide an answer, like a lion scoping out his domain in search of a potential prey. Situations like these tortured me to no end, because I didn't always know how to react. My ambivalence stemmed from a part of me feeling that if I did not maintain eye contact, the teacher would surely sense my weakness and pick me. The other side of me wanted to bluff my way out of it by looking him straight in the eye and project a sense of confidence. An argument ensued in my head over the possibility that my bluff could backfire and earn me a pick. Before I could settle the argument in my head, my teacher had already called me out to answer the question.

My heart was pounding hard, all eyes were on me, and all I wanted was to get my teacher off my back as quickly as possible. Unfortunately, I just didn't know enough English to express my belief that gender was irrelevant as a qualification for the job. I also feared that if I said "Yes," he'd ask me to elaborate further. Fearing of having to further explain my true answer, instead, I replied with a short, snappy answer of "No," and hoped that he'd get off my back.

My quick answer only ignited his curiosity. My teacher looked me straight in the eye and asked, "Why not, Mr. Long?"

Oh boy! Now his second question required an even longer response. Again, I responded with what I thought would get him off my back. I lied and said, "Because they are not good enough."

As soon as those toxic words rolled out of my mouth, the classroom fell into a deafening silence. If looks could kill, the death ray looks aimed at me by my female classmates, would have shred me to pieces many times over. Fortunately, my instigator teacher had decided not to add more fuel to the fire and finally moved on to another topic.

I was really struggling with the language and cultural barriers, and felt trapped in my own little world. I couldn't get myself to approach my parents and talk to them about the difficulties I was experiencing. Even if I spoke English well, I wouldn't know how to go about having a meaningful dialogue with my parents over the cultural struggles that I, myself, did not understand. Given that I wasn't saying anything about what was on my mind, my parents probably assumed that everything was fine. Or maybe, they too, simply did not know how to handle a confused teenager.

In their own way, my parents tried to be as supportive as they could be. They gave me a lot of space, both physical and psychological. Perhaps the private space I received was too much for me to handle. It made me feel as though my parents were keeping their distance from me. The truth is, I could have really used some guidance at that point in my life, but I didn't know how to go about attaining it. My frustrations boiled over and manifested into other negative forms. I began to harbor resentments towards my parents, and copped a rebellious attitude for not being the perfect parents that I had expected them to be.

During my phase of teenage defiance, I discovered two important facts about my parents. One was that they are only human, and not the super humans I once thought they were. They made mistakes and were susceptible to mood swings just like I was. The second discovery I made was that my actions hurt them. I started doing things I knew would not please them, like talking back to my mom. I learned this behavior from watching my American friends who always talked back to their parents. My attitude undoubtedly created tension in my home.

Mom's Filipino method of handling conflicts was one that I was too familiar with. When my mother was offended, she would not talk to the person about the offense. Instead, she would quietly shun and ignore the offender as her way of getting even and letting it be known that a line had been crossed. Filipinos refer to this practice as "excommunication." The practice probably has its roots in religious censures that were originally used to deprive, suspend, or limit membership within a religious community, like the Catholic Church.

My mom's reasoning for such behavior was that it was best to stay quiet in order to prevent creating a bigger problem in the heat of an angry discussion. She felt that it was better to just let an issue go, and wait for the hurt and anger to naturally subside. In the long run, she reasoned, things would eventually work themselves out. The problem with this approach was that anger could linger for days, weeks, months or even years.

I recall a time when my mother and I had a falling out. Rather than openly hashing out the problem, we both automatically locked horns in a battle to see of who could excommunicate the longest. Having been brought up in the same environment as my mother, I was more than willing to play along. When I would get home from school, my mother would lock herself in her bedroom. In response, when she got home from work, I would bolt right out of the house. We lived under the same roof and still avoided each other like a plague.

This folly went on for six months, and neither of us was willing to give in.

The stalemate was finally broken when I infuriated Dad one day. I had come home from school in a foul mood over an argument I had with the girl who I was dating at the time. It was a fight that continued over the telephone when I arrived home. My girlfriend would call, we'd argued, and I'd slammed the phone; a cycle that repeated several times.

Dad, who was tinkering in the garage, poked his head-in through the doorway to see what the commotion in the kitchen was all about. He saw me talking on the phone having a miltdown. Calmly, he asked, "Could you please keep it down? Your mother is sleeping."

When I heard him say that, I completely lost it. I violently slammed the telephone against the receiver and did it repeatedly. Dad came in the house and followed me as I marched to my mother's bedroom. I started banging my fist on her bedroom door, yelling, "What do you care? This bitch doesn't give a shit. And what are you going to do about it, kick me out of your house?"

I started kicking the hallway walls and punctured holes in it. Dad came over and bear hugged me, dragged me to the front door, and pushed me out. He told me to take a walk and cool off, to which I childishly replied, "Too late Dad, I'm out of here! I hate this place! I'm never coming back!"

I took the bus to San Bernardino Mall, twenty miles away, to figure out my next move. A few minutes after I arrived at the mall, I felt a discomfort in my right ankle. I bent down to take a look and saw that it had swollen up like a balloon. The discomfort quickly turned into an agonizing pain. I had twisted my ankle when I kicked the hallway walls and not realized it. I hopped to the nearest phone booth and called Dad for help. Bill, of course, without question or hesitation, wasted no time and came to my rescue.

Only then did I have the courage to approach my mother and break the silence that had gripped us for so long. I apologized for my despicable behavior and for all of the ugly things I had said to her. Tearfully, she accepted my apology, and acknowledged that she could have also done a better job defusing the situation at her end before it got out of hand.

This episode with my mother taught me that I needed to reevaluate the way I instinctively managed conflict. I had been apart from Mom for most of my life, and I had just wasted six long months by giving her the silent treatment. I should have spent every precious moment with Mom to make up for all those years we had lost. I was approaching my eighteenth birthday and was well aware that my time with the family would soon come to an end. I vowed to handle conflict differently from that moment on, and make better use of the remaining time we had.

In the spring of 1979, my dad travelled back to the Philippines to bring my sister Gina over, just as he had done for me four years prior. My sisters' arrival marked the reunification of our entire family. For the first time in our lives, all four of my mother's children were finally together. Gina arrived in April, and fortunately, my parents did not send her to school right away. This decision gave her a few months to adjust to her new environment. My presence also made it a little easier for my sister, because we could speak in our dialect and I could provide answers to any of her questions. When she resumed her schooling in August, Gina was a little more accustomed to the transition than I had been.

My high school years were winding down rapidly, and my immediate concern was to graduate with the rest of my class. My attendance was so poor that I wasn't sure if I could graduate on time. I knew playtime was over; it was time for me to step-up and get serious with my responsibilities. I would have to work twice as hard to make up for the years I had spent neglecting my studies. *Education was a necessity if I wanted to have a better future*, I told myself. My plan was to graduate from high school and sign-up for a three-year-tour in the US Army, in order to gain some work experience, and travel the world.

In the summer of that same year, I met the person who would ultimately alter the course of my life. Her name was Erika James. I met her at a local disco bar called Porky's Club. It was the only disco club in town and a favorite hangout for teenagers. I've always been fond of dancing, and the place offered a friendly environment for kids to have good, clean fun. It even had an elevated, multi-colored lit dance floor similar to the one in "Saturday Night Fever," a popular movie at the time.

I have heard, but never paid attention to the notion of love at first sight. However, that evening, I felt an instant connection the moment I laid eyes on Erika. My gut feeling told me that this person was going to play a major role in my life. Her presence represented a familiar sense, as though we had spent a whole lifetime together in the past. I instantly thought of my so called "better half" that Grandma Rufina fondly spoke of in her stories.

A classmate soon introduced us, and Erika and I, despite my thick Filipino accent, instantly established a strong bond. We clicked like long lost friends reuniting after a lengthy separation. Neither of us had a car, so I offered to walk her home when the club closed. She agreed, and we talked non-stop all the way to her grandmother's house, where she lived at the time. We learned that we had many things in common, like how miserable we felt living at home with our parents. Erika did not get along with her step-father, to the point where she felt she had no other choice but to run away from home. Unlike me, who just bluffed about running away, Erika had actually done it. However, when Erika wanted to return home, her parents no longer welcomed her. And that's how she ended up living with her grandparents, who happened to live just a few blocks away from my parents' home.

With Erika, I didn't have to worry about her making fun of the way I talked, which was a big deal to me. I felt so comfortable with her that I found myself talking freely about all the difficulties I was going though in my life, and all the while, she listened attentively. The conversation transitioned to talks about our fears, our dreams, and how life would be if we had it our way. Before either of us could prepare to end the evening, we were already standing at her grandmother's door step. We shook hands and made plans to see each other again the next day.

Throughout the long, hot summer that year, Erika became my constant companion. We both applied for part time jobs; she at a fast food restaurant and I at a nursery garden. We spent every cent of what little we earned on fast food, movies, and days at the parks. Before long, Erika became a familiar face to my family.

When I introduced Erika to Mom, she, like most Americans, addressed my mother by her first name - Yoly, short for Yolanda. She didn't know it, but Erika had just disrespected my mother. Though my mother had already lived in America for years, she still operated under the Filipino cultural mentality. Erika addressing Mom by her first name offended her tremendously, but predictably, my mother kept it to herself and never corrected my girlfriend. As Erika continued to address Mom as "Yoly", my mother kept her distance from her.

In contrast, Erika's grandparents welcomed me instantly to their family. I referred to them fondly as Grandma Stack and Grandpa Red. I would often hang around their place and enjoy Grandma Stack's home cooked meals. Erika's grandfather worked as a truck driver at a moving company and would occasionally hire me as a part-time worker. It was back-breaking work of heavy lifting, but Grandpa Red compensated me fairly. Her grandparents liked having me around. They figured if we were home, we would have less time to get ourselves into trouble, but sometimes, trouble happened when its least expected.

A case in point was when I was walking home late one evening from Erika's place. We had spent the afternoon target practicing in her grandparents' back yard using my BB pistol. It was only a pellet gun, but it looked very much like a real handgun. I had the pistol tucked in my back pocket with its handle prominently visible as I was walking home. It never dawned on me how menacing I must have appeared; looking like a long haired hippie with a handgun sticking out of my back pocket.

I was strutting along the side of an elementary school, carefree as can be, when I suddenly heard the thunderous screeching of tires behind me. I turned and was confronted by a police car that had screeched to a halt in the middle of the street. Its blinding searchlight shone directly in my eyes, and the two officers were already out of the car with their weapons drawn and aimed right at me. One of them firmly commanded me to, "Get your hands up and don't move!"

I quickly complied, my eyes fixated on the gun pointed right at me. The gun's steel barrel looked pitiless and cold. I froze momentarily, and then it dawned on me that the commotion had been caused by the pellet gun in my back pocket. I proceeded to drop my right hand with the intention of pulling out the fake pistol to show the officers that it was only a toy. Fortunately, the moment I motioned to move my arm, one of the police officers had already made his way to my right - just in time to tackle me down to the ground. I was lucky that the officer got to me before I could act what I had in mind. Undoubtedly, the officers would have reacted in self-defense and shot me. The menacing sight of the gun barrel had distracted me so much that I hadn't seen the other officer sneak up on me and inadvertently save my life.

The officers were relieved to learn that I only had a toy gun in my possession, but they confiscated it anyway. Before they released me, they gave me a long lecture about the danger of what had just happened. Then they told me I could claim my property back at the police station if I wanted to. It took a few minutes as I walked home for it to finally hit me just how close I had been to getting shot. I didn't bother to recover my toy gun.

The incident served as a chilling reminder of how things, in an instant, can quickly turn for the worse. Serving as each other's confidants, Erika and I strived to make positive changes in our lives. She believed that if we were to build a long lasting relationship, it was necessary to disclose certain things about her, she felt I should know. I agreed, and as we sat on my parents' front lawn one afternoon, she tearfully revealed that she had been a victim of incest.

At nine years old, Erika had been sexually molested by her father's brother. If that wasn't tragic enough, at age thirteen, she was subsequently raped by her father. The deplorable revelation made me sick to my stomach. I had no idea that such unforgivable acts could actually exist. I was speechless in the presence of a devastated young woman whose life had only just begun. I didn't know what to say. I just held her in my arms as she wept. Her disclosure only strengthened the bond we had. She trusted me with her most intimate secret and I was determined to protect her from the monsters in the world; to be her "knight in shining armor."

Summer came to an end, and it was time to finish my final year of high school. I embraced the new school year with a sense of purpose. Four years had gone by since my arrival in the United States, and my English had noticeably improved. Though I still couldn't express my thoughts fluently, I could understand most of what was being said and, somewhat, respond accordingly. With this improvement, I was determined to take my studies seriously.

I met with my school counselor, who explained the steps I needed to take to graduate with the rest of the senior class. To make up for the lost times, I had to take several early bird and evening classes, on top of my regular curriculum. I willingly complied and did so with enthusiasm.

I breezed right through my first semester and passed all of my classes, which boosted my self-confidence. Now that I could grasp what was being taught, attending all my classes became an enjoyable experience; I was actually learning. No one on my mother's side of the family had ever graduated from high school before, and I sought to be the first. I wanted my family, especially Grandma Rufina, to be proud of me. From my perspective, everything was falling in place and, for the first time, the future looked promising.

Erika, on the other hand, attended a different kind of school; a prep school for the GED exam. The program was designed to help troubled students earn their high school equivalent diploma. The prep school was conducted inside a government building next to my school and was attended by students who had been expelled from regular schools. Because of the close proximity of our schools, Erika and I would meet for lunch every day. Like clockwork, she would always wait for me at her school's parking lot and we'd walk across the street to a fast food restaurant.

One day, I found Erika crying when I met her at our usual spot. A boy in her class had taunted her and called her some unflattering names. Without thinking, I barged into the classroom and interrupted the ongoing study session. Erika pointed toward the far end of the room, where the culprit was kneeling down by the bookshelves. As we approached, he stood up with a taunting smirk on his face. I was livid and demanded, "Let me hear you call my girlfriend a bitch."

He replied, "I didn't call her a bitch."

His condescending tone, along with the silly smirk on his face, got the best of me, and impulsively, I pelted him in the face with a right hook. The boy fell to the floor, created a commotion and causing the teacher to call security. The police came in minutes, but they did not arrest me; instead, I was instructed to go back to class and report to the principal's office later. Erika and I went on to lunch, proud to have taught that bully the consequences of picking on a young woman. Admittedly, I felt like I had just brought down a villain. I didn't have the faintest idea of the severity of what I had done.

That afternoon, I was ushered to the principal's office, where I learned the hard news that I was no longer welcome at Fontana High School. The principal told me to clear out my locker that very day and said that I should be thankful that the boy's parents did not want to press charges against me.

I couldn't believe the harshness of my punishment. I pleaded for a second chance and explained that I had to stay in school to fulfill my promise to my grandmother. Sadly, there was no second chance. The principal was set on making his point and adamantly carried on with his decision. He would only say that I should have thought about the consequences before pulling a "John Wayne move" in his school.

In an instant, my well-thought-out plans had been derailed, and the future looked bleak. I didn't lay the blame on Erika, because it was I who had decided to act out of anger. I didn't have the courage to tell my parents what had happened, so I tried to hide it from them. Day after day, I pretended to be in school, but they eventually found out the truth. I had let my parents down, and I could see it in their eyes. I imagined Grandma Rufina having that same disappointed look in her eyes when she learns the news of the incident. The thought of it, ripped me apart inside.

Shortly after that terrible incident, I had another life-changing surprise - Erika was pregnant. We had only known each other for six months and had carelessly engaged in unprotected sex. My reaction when she told me the news was a telling sign of my immaturity: "How can that be?"

A month or so after the announcement of her pregnancy, Erika's grandmother urged her to move back in with her mother and step father, whom by then, had relocated to the state of Michigan. Sensing that she had worn out her welcome at her grandma's home, Erika reluctantly agreed.

The idea of simply walking away from my obligations to Erika crossed my mind when she left. She was far away, and no one at home was pressuring me to do anything about the situation. In the privacy of my own thoughts, however, I could not ignore the fact that a child I had helped create was about to be brought into this world. I struggled with the decision of what to do, and spent long hours carefully weighing the pros and cons of the situation.

After mulling it over for weeks, in the final analysis, I made the decision to face up to my responsibility and do right by Erika. It was the moral thing to do, and I was certain that Grandma Rufina would approve of my decision. I informed my parents that I was going to marry Erika and join the military. After I told them of my plan, neither of them was jumping for joy. Dad insisted we have a talk. He took me in his pick-up truck with a six pack of beer and drove to the local park.

Dad tried to persuade me to reconsider. He reasoned that getting married was not my only option, and I could still be a part of my child's life by providing child support. He expressed his concern that despite our close bond, the fact remains that Erika and I really did not know each other well enough to get married. He added that I could always marry Erika further out in the future, when I was absolutely certain that she was the one for me. Dad pleaded for me to give it time, and not make a hasty decision to get married out of obligation.

From my point of view, walking away from my paternal responsibility was not an option. I knew I was completely unprepared to take on the role of a father, but I wanted to give my child the privilege of being raised by her biological parent. It's a desire I had for my child that trumped all of the plans I had for myself.

I grew up knowing the feeling of abandonment all too well. I could not eloquently explain to Dad the sadness I felt when none of my parents could represent me during parent-teacher meetings in grade school. I couldn't adequately describe to him the mixed feelings of rejection and admiration I had, as I enviously watched my classmates enter the room with both parents in hand. The feeling was all too familiar to me, and I could not in good conscience let my child experience the same emptiness I had felt in my formative years. I firmly said to Dad my decision was final, and that perhaps someday I might do a better job of explaining my reasons.

A few days after our talk, Dad drove me to the military recruiter's office, where I signed up to join the US Army. I was well aware of my lack of education, that I spoke with a thick Filipino accent, and didn't know much of anything about the ways of the real world. I only knew that I will be a father soon; a colossal responsibility to fill. Anything else, I'd have to figure out as I come across it along the way.

The hard feelings I once harbored for my parents' short comings seemed trivial now that time was running out. I wished I could have done a better job of letting my family know how much they meant to me, and how fortunate I felt to have them in my life. Such powerful insight only came into focus upon the realization that I was about to leave the comfort and safety of my family's home. How I wished I could stay just a little while longer, but the tide of change had once again arrived at my door step. I'd have to come to terms with what was, and do a better job of strengthening my relationship with my parents in the future.

CULTURE CLASH

On April 14, 1980, Erika and I wed in a small ceremony held in her parents' backyard in Michigan. The following month, I flew back to California and reported for duty to the United States Army on May 27, 1980.

CHAPTER 7

THE DARK SIDE OF UNCONDITIONAL LOVE

"Consider how hard it is to change yourself and you'll understand what little chance you have in trying to change others."

- Jacob M. Braude

***

The notion of "unconditional love" was one of the most challenging aspects of my Filipino heritage to rise above. In her unassuming way, Grandma Rufina had bestowed upon me the magic of this precious gift. Through her actions, I had come to embrace this ideal as an iron clad rule: Reciprocate love unconditionally. For so long, I held onto this belief with reverence, and blindly did so, until I found myself in a situation that caused me to question this concept. Up until then, it had never occurred to me to even consider that there might be negative aspects to such an uncompromising stance.

The moment we descended from the bus and into the hot, muggy weather of Fort Jackson, South Carolina, we were greeted by the man who was going to be our mom and dad for the next six weeks: the drill sergeant. I stood in formation with the rest of the new recruits, stiff as an ironing board and praying for this angry man not to single me out in front of everyone.

I suppose my appearance was too much of an oddity for the drill sergeant to resist. I was nineteen years old, standing at attention in blue jeans, a Van Halen t-shirt, and thick black hair that dangled down to my back. I was the only Asian in the group, and looking like a rock star on a budget. Much to my horror, this deranged man suddenly came just inches away from my face. He stared me right in the eye and yelled at the top of his lungs, "What are you looking at, rock star wannabe?"

The absurdity of a grown man eyeballing me and asking what I was looking at, made me chuckle, and my reaction turned this beast from belligerent to outright nuts. "Are you laughing at me, Rock Star?"

I snapped, "No, Sergeant!"

"Then you must be laughing at life, Rock Star! Let me tell you something about life… I can't hear you, Rock Star!"

"Yes, Sergeant!"

"The only thing you need to remember, Rock Star, is that life is like a dick! Do you know why that is, Rock Star?"

"No, Sergeant!"

"Life is like a dick, Rock Star, because when it's soft, you can't beat it, and when it's hard, it gets fucked! "

He backed away from me and turned to the rest of the platoon, "And that goes for all of you little maggots! Life for you is going to be an absolute dick for the next eight weeks in my boot camp!"

That was my refreshing introduction to life in the U.S. Army. I spent the entire summer of 1980 in Fort Jackson, where I completed Basic Training and schooling for my occupation in the military as Food Service Specialist. I was still insecure about my English and did not want to jeopardize my livelihood by taking on a job that was more than I could intellectually handle. I aspired to become a certified chef, so getting the experience in

Food Service while in the military made sense to my objective. I figured, besides getting training for my chosen field, how complicated could food preparation be?

I quickly discovered that my chosen profession was actually one of the most demanding jobs in the Army. The work itself was not very difficult; I took pleasure in food preparation and the satisfaction of seeing the soldiers enjoying their meals. The problem was that there were never enough cooks in Uncle Sam's Army. Consequently, cooks had to work longer hours than most soldiers.

My standard schedule was to work twelve straight days, followed by two days off. There were no breaks on holidays. In fact, cooks had to work even longer hours during holidays, especially Thanksgiving and Christmas. Typical shift duration was ten hours on weekdays and twelve on weekends. I soon realized that working in Food Service was a thankless job in the military.

Soldiers who were disqualified from other lines of work for misbehaving, were reclassified as military cooks as their punishment. Indeed, the staggering amount of hours I spent slaving away in the kitchen felt like a punishment. Despite the long hours at work during my four months training at fort Jackson, I did manage to pass my G.E.D. exam and receive an equivalent high school diploma.

I arrived at the Aberdeen Proving Ground in Maryland in the fall of 1980. The way I ended up in Maryland for my first duty assignment was a bit of a farce. When I signed up for the military in California, I was given the option to choose my first duty station. The choices included Japan, Germany, Panama, Korea, and several bases within the continental United States.

When I saw Maryland on the list, I thought it was a foreign country. It matched the names of European countries like England, Scotland, Finland, and Ireland. So I automatically assumed it was just another country name that ended with "land."

After I signed the contract to join the military, the recruiter firmly shook my hand and congratulated me for coming on board. Out of sheer curiosity, I asked the recruiter what language was spoken in Maryland. He thought I was joking at first, but when I persisted, he realized I was actually serious.

The sergeant tried to keep a straight face as he led me back to his office. He pointed to a map that was posted on the wall behind his desk. He carefully explained that it was a map of the United States, and then pointed to the state of Maryland.

To say that I was embarrassed would be an understatement. The sergeant must have thought I was an idiot. Even worse, seeing my hair almost down to my waist, he probably thought I was on drugs. I asked if I could switch the location to Germany instead, but he politely explained that it was too late.

Aberdeen was a small town, twenty-six miles from Baltimore. Erika and I, along with our newborn baby, Rena, would spend my term in the military there. My meager salary of $700 per month forced Erika and I to put every dime toward making ends meet.

As a low-ranking soldier, a Private, my name was at the bottom of the military base housing list. We had no other option but to rent a one-bedroom apartment outside the post for $140 per month until military housing became available. With so little money, buying a car was out of our reach. Instead, I depended on a ten speed bicycle to get me back and forth from work.

My shift started at 4:30 a.m. I'd pedal my heart out for 45 minutes to get to work on a poorly lit road that cut across a wooded area to the military base. It was a long, strenuous ride that became even more challenging during the winter months.

Coming from a tropical island where temperatures hardly ever dipped below seventy degrees, I was not prepared for the winter. I had to pedal my way through an icy road in freezing temperatures before the break of dawn every morning. Given that I didn't know anyone in town and had no family members to call on for assistance, there was really no other choice but to make do with what I had. Despite the difficulties, I rolled out of bed each day, went to work, and diligently did my job.

Having experienced for myself the hard work it took to provide for a family made me appreciate the easy life I had at home with my parents. They made running a household seem so effortless - all the bills were paid, groceries were readily available, provided roof over my head, and they never complained. My blue collar parents met their obligations head-on, while I bitched and moaned.

Christmas came, and unfortunately, I had to work the usual grueling holiday shift from 4:30 a.m. to 8 p.m. Erika, all the while, was stuck at home alone with the baby, we didn't even owned a television to keep her company. She patiently waited at home the whole day. I was flat broke and couldn't afford to buy my wife a Christmas present. It didn't feel right to come home empty-handed on what should be a festive occasion. As a last resort, I sold the most valuable possession I had: my only pair of gloves.

I sold my gloves for five dollars to my colleague, the dish washer, who also rode his bicycle to work. On my way home, I stopped at a convenience store to find a small present for my wife. It was well past 9 p.m. when I finally arrived home. Erika greeted me with a surprise Christmas dinner laid out on the table: pot roast, mashed potatoes, corn on a cob, and candied yams. She had prepared everything by herself.

I handed her the paper bag I held in my hand and wished her a Merry Christmas. Excitedly, she opened the brown bag that contained two sets of colorful drinking glasses. It was the only item in the store that I could afford to buy as a gift. Erika knew our money situation, and did not expect to receive anything for Christmas. The little gift I had, delightfully made her cry. We feasted at the dinner table and quietly enjoyed what remained of our first family Christmas together.

Several months passed, and we managed to save up $500 to buy an old blue 1969 Chevrolet Impala. It needed lots of repairs and was a gas guzzler, but it kept me warm in the winter months and enabled the family to go places. Slowly, Erika and I adapted to life of being on our own, though we struggled to make ends meet most of the time. Having been married at such a young age and deprived ourselves of all the fun that youthful indiscretions supposed to bring, our curiosities made us especially susceptible to the lure of a youthful lifestyle.

The friends we made, like us, were also very young but mostly single. Their company was a welcome break from my all-consuming work routine. We wanted to be around them all the time, but couldn't with a baby in tow, nor could we afford a steady baby sitter. As a compromise, we brought the parties to our apartment instead. We were very trusting and naively welcomed anyone who wanted to join the fun, even people we didn't really know. If they seemed cool to us, it was good enough.

Callously, we partied until the wee hours of the night, with complete disregards to other families in the neighborhood. There were even times when I had to leave for work while the party was still going on in my apartment. Sleep-deprived and physically exhausted, the twelve hour shifts seemed like infinity. This phase of happy-go-lucky living went on for approximately a year. I never saw coming, the potential consequence that our open-door policy could bring.

Then one day, I was approached by a co-worker who informed me that, on his way to work that morning, he had seen my wife and child parked in front of a nearby barracks. I quickly brushed off his allegation, contending that it was simply impossible because Erika had been sound asleep when I left the house before the break of dawn. In the days that followed, I heard similar claims from other colleagues. I continued to ignore their assertions because I had already discussed it with Erika, who vehemently denied it. I trusted my wife wholeheartedly, and it was all I needed to hear.

My faith in our relationship began to loosen-up when Erika started to spend more and more time out with her girlfriends, that gradually extended later and later into the night. My trust unraveled when I came home late Saturday afternoon, after a long weekend shift, and Erika was nowhere to be found. She dropped-off our child to the neighbor next-door, without leaving a note of where she was going, who she was with, or when she was coming back.

Midnight came, and I still had not heard from Erika. By then, I was deathly worried that something terrible had happened to her; it was so unlike her not to call or leave a note. Finally, at around two in the morning, Erika came tip-toeing into the house. She was surprised to see me still wide awake, considering I had another long shift at work the following day.

Erika acted defensive and shifty when asked about her evening's whereabouts. Her evasiveness only increased my suspicions, which quickly denigrated the conversation into a huge argument. Only after a prolonged heated fight did Erika finally confess that she had been having an affair with a young trainee named Brad.

It broke my heart hearing those words rolling out of her lips. I had demanded the truth, and now that it has been revealed, I wished I hadn't. The truth carried a pain far greater than the nagging hurt of suspicion. At that moment, I felt like the world's biggest fool – violated and defiled.

Erika acknowledged that she had too much time on her hands and had succumbed to temptation. She remorsefully admitted her wrong doing, rendered her apologies, and begged to be forgiven. Tearfully, she promised to make things right again if I would only give her another chance.

I found that in moments like these, when everything that mattered most to me was on the line, I instinctively held onto the things I knew to be true - the deep seated Filipino belief in "sacrifices and forgiveness."

Scenes of the many sacrifices, that Grandpa Antonio had endured just to be with Grandma Rufina, repeatedly played in my head. It was a battle that to Grandpa, as it is for me, was worth fighting for. I found strange consolation in the thought that unlike the monstrous Anastacio who had stood in Grandpa's way, the only obstacle I had to overcome was my pride. To surpass the hurdle, I reassured myself that everything will be alright, once I get passed my wounded heart and battered pride. Undeniably, I remain a product of my Filipino upbringing; a culture that viewed self-sacrifice and forgiveness as virtues to embrace.

I heard what I needed to hear from Erika, and all was forgiven. Leaving the pain of betrayal behind me was not an easy feat. Brad dined in the mess hall where I worked. It was humiliating having to prepare and serve a meal to the man who had an affair with my wife. Each time we came face to face over the counter, my hands shook with rage. To keep myself from leaping over the counter and ripping his head off, I would divert my focus on my two year old daughter. Seeing Rena in my mind's eye helped calm me down.

Unfortunately, things at home showed no improvement. Time and time again, Erika would test the limit of my resolve. She had severe mood swings that often caused heated arguments where she would storm out the door and not come home. After a couple of days, she'd finally call and I would pick her up at various places; sometimes at motels. It took everything in me to compose myself and not lose it altogether.

Eventually, Brad completed his training at Aberdeen Proving Ground and relocated to a duty station far away. I thought everything would be okay again now that he was out of the picture. Unfortunately, her infidelity was only a prelude of the madness that would follow.

Erika was insanely jealous, and we would constantly argue because of it. As ridiculous as it may sound, and considering her infidelity, my saying hello to a female colleague at a super market was grounds for a fight that would last for days. Ironically, she distrusted my every move despite the fact that it was she who had lied and cheated. She must have convinced herself that since she had committed adultery, then I must be doing it also.

Another aspect that made life difficult was Erika's inability to get along with other people, especially with other women. We ended up moving every year during the four-year span of our life in Aberdeen. It was always the same cycle with her - we'd move to a new neighborhood, inevitably Erika gets in a fight, and we'd relocate to avoid the headaches.

We had our tires flattened, seen an angry mob of people at our front door, had gotten into shouting matches with husbands, and were even involved in a court case that dragged on for a couple of years. Life with Erika was very difficult to say the least.

Perhaps the most destructive of Erika's many vices was her dismissive attitude towards higher learning. My substandard salary and the hardship I had to endure in my line of work made me realize the importance of a good education. I wanted to go back to school. I figured earning a college degree, would improve my chances of landing a better job, thus allowing me to spend more time and adequately provide for my family.

Enthusiastically, I shared my grand plan with my wife thinking she would be thrilled and supportive of it. Instead, I got the opposite reaction. Erika had the twisted idea that my pursuit for higher leaning was just a smoke screen, and my true motive was to leave her. She alleged, "You just want to be educated, so you can leave me!"

I tried reasoning but no amount of logical explanation could reach her. Erika was adamantly opposed to the idea of me going back to school. However, I felt so strongly about it that despite her disapproval, I proceeded with my plan. I signed up for a two-hour evening college course held inside the base twice a week. I hoped that when Erika saw how much effort I'd put into this goal, she'd see that my intentions were good and lend me her support. Unfortunately, Erika mistook my initiative as a declaration of war.

Each time I'd come home from class, the house would be a mess, no food on the table, and met with a constant barrage of the same insecure arguments. I hung tough, hoping she'd come to appreciate my efforts and cut me some slack. Erika was relentless in her aim to derail me, which in due course wore me down.

My resistance was breached when one of our intense arguments dragged on for so long that I completely lost track of time. In the middle of our still heated argument, I suddenly realized that it was already 4:15 a.m., and I had to be back at work again at 4:30 a.m.

I hadn't gotten a minute of sleep, nor had I eaten. In fact, I was still wearing my uniform from the day before. Her parting words to me as I hurriedly left for work were, "I hope you fucking die."

The endless battle with my wife proved to be too taxing. Reluctantly, I gave in and dropped out of school.

Similarly, the opportunity I had to pursue my passion in a Culinary Arts competition was met with the same fate. Once a year, the U.S. Army sponsors a Culinary Arts competition at Fort Lee, Virginia, where the top cooks from U.S. military installations from all around the world competed to show case their culinary talents and expertise. The man in charge of my dining facility, Sergeant Welks, saw the potential in my artistic ability and thought I'd make a good addition to the base's Culinary Arts Team. With Sergeant Welks' highly favorable recommendation, I was instantly accepted to the team that would represent Aberdeen Proving Grounds in the upcoming competition. However, being part of the culinary team required extra hours per week in addition to my regular working hours. Predictably, this did not bode well with Erika, and once again, I had to pass up on an opportunity to excel.

There was also a time when I started keeping a personal journal as a way to help improve my communication skill. Chronicling the day's event on paper forced me to organize and articulate my thoughts in English. It was a practice that I found invaluable. Erika knew about the journal and would invade my privacy with complete disregard. She'd read it while I was at work, and would always find something in it to fight about.

No matter where I hid my journal, Erika always managed to find it and start an argument over its content. At times, the squabble had gotten so unbearable that it occurred to me to be less truthful in my journal entries in order to avoid the fights. I had to literally lie to my own diary to avoid any disputes with my wife. It denigrated to a point where Erika would actually write her own comments on it, like an editor would. She'd write things like, "Bullshit! I don't believe you."

The situation was so pathetic that it was almost comical. After giving up so many other things for Erika, her intrusiveness got the best of me again and my enthusiasm for journal writing slowly faded away.

Three years into the marriage, it was apparent that life with Erika was becoming more agonizing by the day. At the same time, I had become exceedingly unhappy with my occupation due to its long hours and redundant work. Ironically, the only solace I could find from my hellish existence was the short commute I had from home to work. I dreaded arriving too soon at either end of my commute. I would have welcomed the long, arduous traffic jams of Los Angeles just to prolong my peaceful ride between the two hells. I remember thinking, *There has got to be more to life than this shit.*

I was angry, not only because of the bleak reality of my situation, but also at my inability to articulate my frustrations, discontentment, and hopelessness. In addition to my struggles with English, I had always found it extremely difficult to express my opinions candidly - not just to Erika, but to anyone, especially in a public setting. I somehow viewed that expressing how I truly felt was a violation of some sacred, unwritten rule. Getting myself to render an honest opinion or openly disagree with anyone was impossible. I was always afraid of making waves and risking offending anyone. I hadn't figured out that my Filipino collectivist mentality was in conflict with American individualist mindset. Not knowing the source of my confusion, prompted me to often take things personally.

In the mist of my unhappy situation, I received an unexpected call from California that would permanently alter my perception on life. We had just finished our supper that evening, and Erika was getting Rena ready for bed. I was in the kitchen putting the dishes away when the phone rang. Mom was on the other line, sobbing profusely. "Benjie?"

I answered, "Mom, are you all right? What's the matter?"

Her voice quivered. "Your Grandma is gone. She passed away yesterday."

CULTURE CLASH

The shock of Grandma Rufina's death, struck me like a bolt of lightning. Silently, I placed the telephone on the dining table and walked to the bedroom, where I curled up in bed and wept like a child. An hour or so later, I heard Erika open the door behind me. She paused without saying a word, then gently closed the door and allowed me to grieve in private.

What began as just another ordinary day turned out to be a tragic day of epic proportions. The problems and dissatisfactions I may have had prior to that dreadful call paled in comparison to the devastating loss that engulfed me. At twenty-one, full of life and boundless energy, I had always believed that Grandma Rufina would always be there for me. I relied on the assumption that there will always be ample time to make up for the years we've missed.

I grappled with the enormity of such a loss and was astonished by the magnitude of death's unforgiving and permanent ways. All along, I thought I was someone special, believing there was somebody up there always looking-out for me and to those I love. But death, I learned too late, didn't discriminate. It descended and took what it came for; swiftly, coldly, and without mercy. Grandma's death brought the humbling realization that I was merely one among billions of temporary inhabitants on earth – that time, had only trivial regard to my wants and wishes.

With Grandma Rufina's passing, gone were the moments that could never be: the letters I could have written, the calls I would have made, and the things I should have said to let her know just how much she meant to me.

I recalled the last time I heard Grandma's voice over the telephone. I had answered a long-distance collect call from her. It had been four years since I left the Philippines, and I had not written or called her since. When the call went through, she recognized my voice and asked, "Do you remember me?"

Nonchalantly I replied, "But of course, Grandma. Here's Mom."

I thoughtlessly handed the telephone to my mother and ran off to whatever it was that occupied my interest at the time. As it turned out, that was the last chance I had to speak with Grandma Rufina and I had callously passed up the opportunity. In retrospect, I could only shake my head in disbelief at how heartless and cold I must have seemed. Because I didn't do any of the things I could have done when I had the chance, a lingering doubt nagged inside my head, *Did Grandma know how much I loved her?*

I couldn't say with certainty that she did, and it bothered me.

Grandma Rufina had once asked of me to attend her funeral, wherever I may be, and place a thin black veil over her face. I promised her that I would. But for reasons that are now foggy to me, I made the choice not to attend Grandma's funeral. Perhaps I did not want to accept the reality that she was really gone, or maybe I couldn't get myself to face Grandma after failing her in so many ways. I carried a colossal burden of guilt in my failure to keep in touch, the letdown of not being able to graduate from high school, my inability to have a successful career path, and the struggle I had to keep my marriage from falling apart. These reasons, along with whatever excuses I had, prevented me from fulfilling a solemn oath I made. I had broken yet another promise - a decision I would live to regret.

Despite the enormity of my loss, I didn't have the luxury of mourning longer than I needed to. Responsibilities at work and home required my full attention. To Erika's credit, she refrained from complicating the situation further during my time of bereavement. In the ensuing months, we quietly pieced together the fragments of our broken relationship. Grandma's loss had taught me just how fragile life and everything in it can be. I gained a renewed sense of appreciation for people in my life; never again will I take their presence for granted.

In the spring of 1983, Erika together with our daughter visited her family, who had relocated from Michigan to Oklahoma City. It was a trip that was long over-due and one that Erika had been looking forward to. We couldn't afford plane fare for the three of us, so I agreed to pass up this trip and remained at home.

One week into what was supposed to be a two week vacation, I received a frantic call from Erika that she was coming home. She alleged that her stepfather, whom I'd come to know and respect, had sexually assaulted her. Erika recounted that she and her stepfather had driven home together in his work van, when he suddenly took a detour to an isolated location and attempted to have his way with her. Although, Erika was able to persuade him to stop, his actions had already triggered memories of sexual abuses inflicted on her by other family members.

Some of the details of Erika's story were unclear, but I could tell by the sound of her trembling voice that she was on the verge of having a mental breakdown. I didn't press for further clarification; I figured there would be plenty of time later to get a better understanding of what had happened. My immediate concern was for my wife and daughter to get home safely.

When I picked them up at the airport twenty-four hours later, Erika's zombie-like demeanor was a stark contrast to the smiling face I had seen the previous week. It baffled me that a man who professed to be a "Born again Christian" could commit such a heinous act. The ripple effect of his exploit left me feeling defiled; this was a man who I looked up to. The contempt I felt was nothing in comparison to how Erika must have felt. I could sense the anguish raging inside by the look in her eyes. As we drove home, the only thing I could do was to silently hold her hand as she leaned back and stared aimlessly out the window.

Getting time off from work was nearly impossible because we were always short of cooks. In light of the gravity of the situation, my Company Commander had granted me one week leave of absence. For several days that followed, Erika stayed curled up in bed, depressed, and seemingly out of reach. I was gravely concerned because she wasn't eating, and I didn't know how long she would remain in this awful condition. I pleaded with her to seek professional help, but she was adamantly against it.

By the week's end, just in time for me to report back to work, she finally emerged from hibernation and showed signs of improvements. She roamed around the house, was eating again, and spending time with Rena. I worried constantly about her being home alone with our daughter. I would often call home to check on her throughout the day.

On the fourth day of being back on shift, I received a call from Harve De Grace Hospital. A staff member from their Mental Health Department informed me that my wife had voluntarily admitted herself to seek treatment. Erika was at the end of her rope, and finally reached-out to seek professional help. Fortunately, a neighbor was willing to lend a hand with our daughter.

I drove to the hospital that evening and met with Erika's doctor. He's diagnosis was that she suffered from a severe form of depression, which will require long-term treatment. The doctor tried to mentally prepare me for the long and rough road ahead of my wife's recovery.

While in treatment, visitations were limited to weekends only and two evening calls during the week. My twelve-on and two-off work schedule meant that I could only visit Erika every other weekend. The prospect of not seeing us for a prolonged period of time was undoubtedly hard for Erika.

Managing the household without her was equally difficult. Her absence was especially hard on our three year old daughter. In order to get to work on time, I would have Rena ready and out of bed at 3:30 a.m. She would remain with the sitter until I got off work late in the afternoons. Rena was always elated to see me coming to bring her home. And by the time I finished feeding, bathing, and tuck my little girls in bed, I'd barely have the energy to do anything else. It was a shared sacrifice that had to be made, and one that I embraced. I knew my wife was getting the proper treatment that had been long overdue.

Unfortunately, Erika didn't quite see it the same way. After having been in the program for only a month, she wanted out. She argued that she was not getting any better, and in fact, the place was driving her even more insane. Legally, Erika could not be forced to remain in treatment against her will; she left the hospital despite her physician's strong opposition. There was nothing that neither the doctor nor I could say or do, to make her change her mind.

Shortly after Erika's return home, we received a telephone call from Oklahoma. At the other end of the line was her stepfather. We had not spoken to him or my mother-in-law since the incident. He made no excuses for what he had done, tearfully apologized, and pleaded for our forgiveness. Given my inclination to be exceedingly forgiving, I readily accepted his apology. Erika, on the other hand, was not easily persuaded. Who could blame her? But eventually, she came around and patched things up with her stepfather. We moved-on with our lives bearing one less burden to carry.

My three year commitment with the military was winding down. Though the dislike I had for my job had grown, I couldn't afford to do away with the steady income and full health benefits that the military provided for my family. At twenty two, my command of the English language was still very poor. I didn't have the self-confidence to go out and strike it on my own in the civilian world. I resorted to rationalizing that, at least in the military, I knew what to expect and, so far, had been able to successfully meet my responsibilities. I felt that I didn't really have much of a choice but to reenlist for another three years, and so I did.

On February 1, 1984, Erika gave birth to our second daughter Niah, just ten months after leaving her mental health treatment. With the addition of a new member to our family, Erika and I made some key changes to our relationship. We did away with our former party friends and only mingled with other married couples. Even the way we dressed reflected the changes in our outlooks and attitudes. When we did run into former friends, they'd often comment, "You guys are all grown up now."

The situation at work also showed signs of improvement. I had been promoted to the rank of a Sergeant and given the responsibility of managing my own shift. The extra income enabled us to put money aside for a down payment on a used car; a white 1980 Chevrolet, Chevette. It had low mileage, fuel efficient, and far more dependable than the big clunker we had. The only concern I had with the Chevette was its size; it wasn't very roomy, and the doors were so slender they reminded me of cardboard. I feared that if we ever got into a serious car accident, our chance of survival was questionable at best. In a way, it was like riding inside a moving coffin. This suspicion was put to the test one day.

I had just dropped Erika off at the bowling alley and was on my way to quickly retrieve something at home and come right-back. I exited the parking lot in a hurry, only to catch the traffic light turn red as I reached the main intersection. It started to drizzle as the light turned green. I flicked my windshield wipers on and drove forward to make a left turn. As I made my way to the middle of a four way intersection, I heard panicky screams and honks from other drivers. I looked to my left and realized a large vehicle had run through a red light and was about to plow into me. From my angle, the truck must have been less than ten feet away, speeding at approximately 100 miles per hour. It seemed there was absolutely no way that the driver could avoid hitting me.

Instinctively, I slammed on the brake with such a force that my car stalled in the middle of the intersection. I heard a loud thud and thought it must have been the impact of the collision, but the car hadn't moved. I exited the vehicle and walked around it to survey the damage - amazingly, the pickup truck had completely missed me. I could only watch in disgust and great relief as the truck's taillights swiftly faded from the scene.

I got back in the car and instead of making a left turn; I drove straight through the intersection and pulled over on the side of the street to regain my composure. I needed to catch my breath, not because of fear or anger, but because during the incident, I had experienced something that was truly astonishing. Right when all of my senses anticipated the impact, I experienced what's commonly known as a *flashback*. I had heard the term before, but I had never experienced it or fully understood what it meant.

The most incredible part of the whole experience was that every waking memory stored in my brain, as far back as I could conceivably recall, replayed in rapid succession before me. I virtually relived every single detail in my twenty-four years of existence: the people I had met, the conversations I've had, and everything I did. All of it played out exactly as they were; chronologically, vividly, and in real time. Astoundingly, every strand of memory was accompanied with all the raw emotions belonging to each recollection. I experienced the full impact of reliving my entire life in the span of a nanosecond, perhaps even less.

The experience was so overwhelming that I had to pull over to calm myself down. My heartbeat pounded so hard that my chest felt like it was about to explode. For many years, I tried to make sense out of the experience. The only plausible conclusion

I could come up with was that, possibly, a flashback is nature's way of diverting our attention at the precise moment when we face our own demise. Perhaps when the mind senses that we are about to take our last breath, it releases a chemical reaction that unleashes a life time of memories that's been tucked away in our memory bank. By cheating death, perhaps I had stumbled onto life's last great surprise.

Still reeling from what I had just experienced, I returned to the bowling alley. I didn't share with Erika and friends what happened – it was too strange and too complicated to explain. No one would've probably believed me anyway. I was too distracted to bowl well the rest of the evening, but it didn't matter. I was just grateful to be there.

At the home front, things had improved considerably. Erika and I didn't engage in senseless fights as much anymore. Naturally, we still had our disagreements, but they were minor and pale in comparison to the destructive fights we used to have. But just when things were shaping up for the better, when least expected, life has an inauspicious way of suddenly throwing a curve ball our way. This time, I was being reassigned to South Korea for a year. It was a change that neither Erika nor I were ready to take on.

Korea was considered a hardship tour, whereby family members were not allowed to accompany service members. Niah had just been born a month before when the orders came down. I was given a three-month notice prior to departure to get my affairs in order. Considering my wife's unresolved mental health issues, the thought of leaving Erika on her own to care for a toddler and a newborn was daunting.

I appealed to my chain of command, on the grounds of the hardship my family would be subjected to in my reassignment. I asked for either a year postponement or a reassignment to another military installation where I could bring my family. Everyone that I've reached out to for help in my chain of command was indifferent to my appeal. The First Sergeant flatly told me that unless I knew someone inside the Pentagon, there was nothing that could be done. I was patronized by the Company Commander by suggesting that one year of separation was not all that bad. I tried to make him understand that one year could seem like infinity to someone suffering from mental illness. He just shrugged as if to say, *Oh well*.

The advice I received from the Mess Sergeant was to accept the inevitable, do my time, and make the necessary arrangements to make life a little easier for my wife and children. I've exhausted all my options which did not bode well in my favor. It seemed the only plausible thing left to do was to prepare for the inevitable. I arranged for my family to remain in the base housing for added security. I entrusted Erika with our finances and diverted most of my salary to her, leaving a miniscule amount for me to get by on while in Korea. I wanted to make sure she and the girls were financially sound in my absence. The plan was for Erika and the girls to remain at Aberdeen Proving Ground while I was away. Upon my return, we would relocate to my next duty station together.

On the eve of my departure, I tossed and turned, unable to get a wink of sleep. I got out of bed and checked on the girls. Rena and Niah were sound asleep, completely oblivious of the crossroad that tomorrow would bring. I quietly shut the door and made my way to the living room. I took down a calendar that hung on the wall and flipped through pages of the days and months that lie ahead. I wished I could skip over to the square that marked the day of my return. I could only hope for the day to come when Erika and I would look back at the next twelve months as a blurred memory of brief separation.

If only life was as simple as wishing one's worries away. The old feeling in my childhood that used to haunt me came creeping in; the helplessness of having no control over my destiny, the not knowing what lies ahead, and the fear of never seeing my family again. Everything was set in motion, and there was no turning back. All we could do was buckle up for the long road ahead and do the best we can to carry on with our plans.

The following morning I packed my duffle bag and made several calls to say goodbye to family and friends. By midday on June 1st, 1984, Erika and the girls took me to Baltimore International Airport for my 2 p.m. departure.

As we waited at the terminal gate for my flight to board, I watched Rena scribbling contentedly in her coloring book. She sat quietly in her beautiful red dress that matched the cardboard crown she had gotten in her Happy Meal. I took a mental picture of her knowing she'd be a year older the next time I'll see my daughter again.

Similarly, the little girl cradled in my arms that could barely hold her head up-right, would be walking and talking the next time I see her. I cringed at the thought of missing the subtle and gradual nuances in my daughters' lives over the course of a year.

I gazed at Erika, who was busily tending to Rena's activity, wondering all the while, *Could she hold things together on her own and stay on track with our plan?* I reached over, patted her on the shoulder, and gave her a reassuring smile that everything is going to be all right.

When the boarding announcement sounded overhead, my sorrow got the best of me and couldn't hold back the tears. Neither of us wanted to let go. We continued to hold on to each other closely until a member of the airline staff quietly notified me that everyone had already been on board, and that it was time for me to go.

From my window seat, I could see Erika and the girls clinging-on to each other tightly. As the plane taxed down the runway, my eyes remained fixed at the blurring distant silhouette. The winds of change had once again carried me through another of life's twists and turns. In my heart I know that I will do whatever it takes to fulfill my part to make it through, a resolve that I firmly believed Erika and I shared.

I had anticipated rough challenges ahead, and Korea did not disappoint. I was stationed at Camp Hovey in Dongducheon, 40 miles north of Seoul, South Korea. Every soldier endured an arduous six day work week, and only had Sundays off. I supposed it was the military's way of keeping soldiers out of trouble. And since I had never had the luxury of having weekends off before, the long schedule didn't affect me at all. However, the challenges of not being with my family and living in an unfamiliar territory required major adjustments.

In times like these, letters meant the world to a soldier far away from home. The highlight of my day was the afternoon "mail call," but to my confusion, I stopped receiving letters from Erika after only three weeks. This was the 1980's, long before cell phones, instant messaging, and Skype were widely available. To place a call, soldiers at the base had to endure long lines as they waited their turn to access the landline. Erika was never home to take my calls, I worried that something had happened to her.

I grew more anxious each passing day as I continued my unsuccessful attempts to reach my wife. Days later, my concerns turned to full blown panic when my call was answered by a recorded message announcing that the telephone number I was trying to reach was no longer in service. At that point, I was totally convinced that something had gone wrong.

I got a hold of Erika's mother in Oklahoma City, who, much to my relief, informed me that Erika and the children were alright and temporarily staying with them. I asked to speak with Erika, but she was out doing errands. In the ensuing days, Erika suspiciously avoided my calls. It took several more days of calling before I finally got Erika on the phone.

I could tell by the tone of her voice that she was not thrilled to hear from me, and before I could say anything beyond, "Hi! How are you?"

Erika had cut me off. "Listen Benjie," she interrupted. "We got married at a very young age and for the first time in my life - I'm free. I like it, and I intend to keep it that way."

I had only been gone a little over a month and could not believe what I was hearing. Stunned and speechless, the only thing I could utter was, "What about me?"

Coldly, she responded, "No guilt trip, please!"

Then she just hung up. I stood inside the phone booth, flabbergasted. At the risk of sounding overly dramatic, at the moment, I did feel like an abandoned child, left on the side of the road. Frantically, I called again and again. Erika refused to take the calls. I was furious, incensed at myself for being so trusting, and angry at my wife for betraying me yet again.

In the subsequent weeks, Erika continued to avoid my calls. To defuse my anger, I buried myself in my work. I couldn't afford to go out and get drunk to drown out my misery because I only allotted a measly hundred dollars to get by on each month. Despite what Erika had done, I didn't put a stop to the pay allotment I had arranged for them, I feared that the children may be harmed by the change.

I kept myself occupied with activities at the recreation center, signed up for work-related correspondence courses, and even volunteered at the local orphanage. On my days off, I would take a couple of orphans out of their dreary home and spend time with them. These children were so easy to please with the little things that we adults take for granted; an afternoon in the park, popcorn and movies, and the good ole American fast food restaurants. The simple joy of being a child I see in their eyes, helped me fill the void of being away from my children.

Adjacent to Camp Hovey was another American military base named Camp Casey. It was a much larger base that had a Culinary Arts program in place. I competed against several aspiring chefs to qualify for a spot on the team. The Division level competition was held at a fancy hotel restaurant in Seoul, South Korea. My individual entry won a gold medal in the center piece category and was even selected as the best overall display in the Novice category. The victory automatically earned me a membership of Camp Casey's 1984-85 Culinary Team.

I had never won a prize in my entire life, and the honor came with a fabulous golden trophy. Camp Casey was also awarded the privilege of representing South Korea, with all expenses paid, at the 10th Annual U.S. Army Culinary Arts Competition in Fort Lee, Virginia, in the spring of 1985.

All of these extracurricular activities provided a diversion from the sad reality of my marriage. I never knew what transpired in Maryland to make Erika abandon our plans. I suspected that it had to do with other men, but rather than being consumed by my suspicions, I made productive use of my time.

Nearly six months into my tour, I received an unexpected "mea culpa" letter from Erika. In the letter, she admitted to having yet another affair, this time with the cable guy. Remorseful expressions, appeal for forgiveness, and promises to make things better again reverberated throughout her plea. She reasoned that the need for us to get past our troubles and move on with our lives was of upmost importance for the sake of the wellbeing of our children.

I wondered, *Why didn't she think of these things before she acted? Was I supposed to just accept, forgive, and forget the brutality of her betrayal?* Erika had made those same promises before that in the long-run proved to be nothing more than false hopes.

Curiously, rather than paying attention to what experience is trying to tell me, instead, the notions of loving unconditionally, giving generously, and always be forgiving - rang loudly in my head. Instantaneously, I found myself reverting back again to the memory of Grandpa Antonio's great sacrifices in his failed-quest to be with Grandma Rufina. Despite all the pain and suffering, every molecule in my body urged me to do the same - the right thing. In the final analysis, I still remain a product of my old cultural conditioning. Against my better judgment, I granted Erika another chance.

I submitted a request for a month long emergency leave of absence, which my Company Commander approved without hesitation. The following day, I flew back to the States to salvage what was left of my marriage. Erika and the children greeted my arrival at the Oklahoma City airport. Rena had just turned four, and Niah was going on nine months and had already learned to walk. We drove home to a two bedroom apartment located in the same complex where her parents lived. Instinctively, we fell right into what used to be our normal routine of prepping the girls for the evening. When the girls were finally in bed, Erika and I then diverted our full attention to the eagerly awaited talk of what transpired in the months that we've been apart.

From my angle, setting across from each other at the dining table, I could see traces of the last few months' challenges in Erika's appearance. She looked older, tired, and had lost some weight. Erika seemed a bit anxious; I reached over and held her hands to calm her down. She opened the conversation with, "Benj, so many things have happened since you left. I don't even know where to begin."

She clasped my hands nervously as she continued. "You know that thing that you never wanted me to have? Well, I was pretty drunk one night and I ended up getting a tattoo. It's here on my breast."

Erika knew that I culturally detested tattoos. Americans view tattoos as a form of self-expression, a body art that wasn't always affiliated with criminal activity. Tattoos, back in the day where I'm from, can only be obtained by serving time in prison. Literally, in the Philippines, tattoos signified that the person had been incarcerated. Perhaps today that perception has changed. Mine, certainly have.

"Show me," I insisted.

She unbuttoned her blouse and slipped her bra strap to the side, exposing her tattoo. Awkwardly, I asked, "Is that supposed to be a portrait of Gumby?"

Erika chuckling as she replied, "No, it's supposed to be a rose. The man I was dating at the time did it."

I shook my head in disbelief. "He must have been really drunk when he did it."

"We both were," she said.

The tattoo bothered me. Its ugly and permanent mark, served as a constant reminder of a dark period in my relationship with Erika. However, if I wanted this marriage to work badly enough, I'll have to find a way to get past this.

"I'm so sorry, Benj."

"Well, it happened, and hopefully, your curiosity has been satisfied."

Timidly, Erika chimed in, "It won't happen again Benj. I promise - but there is another thing that I need to tell you."

I took a deep breath and nodded for her to proceed. "I don't know how else to say this, so I'm just going to say it straight out. I haven't paid any of the bills."

"So we're a little behind on our debt payments, no big deal. We'll catch up." I replied assuredly.

Grimly, she said, "I don't think you understand, Benj. I have not paid any of the bills since you left Maryland. Not one bill in months."

"You mean to tell me that you've not made any payments on anything we owed? Not even the car payment? What did you do with all the money, Erika?" I asked angrily.

"I don't know, I just got carried away! I'm sorry. The car is about to get repossessed. They could come at any time now."

I could only bury my face in the palm of my hands in disbelief. Incredibly, Erika had used all of my hard-earned money to finance the fun she had to go along with her new found freedom. I was livid over the thought that my credit rating, something I had worked so hard to build, had crumbled like a house of cards.

Erika sat there silently, waiting for me to say something. I knew things were bad, but I hadn't anticipated this. I was speechless. It took me a few minutes to absorb the shock before I could regain my composure. After a few minutes, I finally said, "What's done is done. There's nothing we can do now. We'll just have to deal with the creditors when they come."

I didn't have much of a choice but to take the optimistic view that, together, we could rebuild everything that we had lost. Erika's remorse for what happened was visibly obvious; I didn't see the point of making her feel worse. In an attempt to lighten the mood, I suggested, "At least we've gotten our issues out in the open and can move on with our lives."

Unfortunately, Erika wasn't finished just yet. Sheepishly, she continued, "There is one more thing."

Saving the worse for last, she proceeded to drop the big bomb. "I may be pregnant with the cable guy's baby."

"Erika, please tell me you're joking."

"Unfortunately, it's true, Benj. It's no joke."

Just when I thought the news couldn't get any worse, she had managed to up the ante. We went back and forth about what to do with the pregnancy, exploring the pros and cons of every alternative. She was adamant about taking abortion out of the equation, and being raised as a Catholic, it didn't take long to convince me. At the conclusion of our grueling discussion, I ended up agreeing to raise the cable guy's child. To put her mind at ease, I assured her that I would treat the child as my own.

Satisfied with the progress we made, Erika said goodnight and excused herself for the evening. I sat alone in an eerily silent room, astonished at the new low I had denigrated myself in. Months earlier, I would not have been able to stomach the thought of my wife being with another man. But there I was, actually agreeing to raise another man's child. I didn't know whether to laugh, scream, or cry. I couldn't help but notice that deep inside of me was a fatalistic willingness to do whatever it took to keep my family together. It's no wonder I never seem to get a break.

A few days later, Erika had her menstrual period, which eliminated the prospect of her pregnancy. It turned out to be a false alarm.

As Erika accurately predicted, a day after my arrival, the repo man came to repossess the car. We were several months behind on payments and could not afford to pay the missed payments in full. Erika, the children, and I watched as the repo man towed away the best car we'd ever had.

Entrusting my wife to handle our finances had been a costly mistake. I took over the responsibility of managing our finances from then on. I convinced the credit card companies not to report the delinquencies to a collection agency and assured them that payments would be made. Unfortunately, nothing could be said to remove the blemish on my credit rating from automobile repossession.

There was still so much more needed to be done, but my month long stay had already come to an end. It was time for me to go back and serve-out the remaining six months of my tour in Korea. This time around, I wasn't as confident about how things might turn out in my absence. Erika had already demonstrated the devastating havoc that could occur in a short period of time. I had to take a "wait and see" approach, I figured things couldn't possibly get any worse than they already had.

Several weeks after I returned to my post, and shortly before Christmas, I received what we referred to in the military as a "Dear John letter." It came from Erika announcing that she was filing for a divorce. She claimed to have found the man of her dreams and sternly warned me against fighting for custody of the girls. It just came out of nowhere; there was no warning sign, no argument or misunderstanding of any sort. After all of our talks, plans, and promises to work things out, Erika, yet again, had thoughtlessly dismantled any hope of reconciliation. This woman truly believed that I was nothing more than an emotional punching bag. Whatever positive sentiment I had left in our relationship, at that point, had completely unraveled. She had callously trampled on my emotions and utterly disregarded the well- being of children.

Erika wasted no time, and by mid-January, the divorce papers had arrived in the mail. She demanded child support and full custody of our children, but I wasn't about to just roll over and agree to any of it. I sought legal counsel from the Camp's Judge Advocate General, who formally responded to her request and informed her of my intent to battle it out in court.

Three months went by without a word from Erika, and then unexpectedly, I received an urgent message to call my parents in California. I suspected something bad must have happened. My parents would never reach out to me that way unless it was vitally important. I hurried down to the call center.

Mom informed me that in early March, Erika had returned to California and dropped the children off to my parents' house and just disappeared. She didn't say where she was going, who she was with, or when she was coming back for the girls. Mom was concerned that something bad might have happened after not hearing from Erika for weeks. I told her that I couldn't care less what happens to Erika, the only concern I had was for the girls' security.

I may have convinced my mother that I was completely devoid of any feelings for my wife, but secretly, I worried for Erika's safety. The uncertainty of not knowing Erika's whereabouts or the company she was keeping, troubled me deeply. The thought of her turned up dead crossed my mind. How would I explain that to my daughters? Apparently I still cared what happened to Erika, and these worries plagued me throughout my remaining time in Korea.

I was in the middle of finishing my six-week Non-Commissioned Officer Training Course when I finally received another letter from Erika. It was almost a complete replica of her previous "Mea Culpa" letter. She knew how to manipulate my emotions and chose her words cleverly to appeal to my altruistic side, and my innate desire to give the children a happy home. Once again, she took full responsibility for her infidelity, expressed remorse for the pain she had caused, begged for forgiveness, and chattered about the importance of having our family back together again. At the end of her letter, Erika casually added that while out on the road with a man who worked for the circus, she had become addicted to heroin and ended up selling herself on the streets to support her addiction.

Erika's self-destructive ways were bottomless. I cared for her so deeply that whatever pain she inflected on herself, I also felt. She couldn't see the devastation she brought into my life. Erika demanded superhuman strength from me as she took and took, always expecting me to give endlessly. But despite her proven monstrosity, I remained a prisoner of ingrained cultural ideals I couldn't free myself from. I continued to struggle with what should have been an easy call to make. These were the lingering thoughts that occupied my mind as I concluded my tour of duty in South Korea.

I contemplated my next move during the eighteen hour return flight to California. The rational side of me reasoned that Erika's self-destructiveness would always wreak havoc with our marriage, and with her adamant refusal to seek professional help, I could not win a battle that was already lost. Strangely, in spite of the revolting things Erika had done to herself, to our family, and to me, there was still a part of me that was inclined to continue the fight to save our marriage.

Dad picked me up at the airport and during our long commute home, I filled him in on the year long struggle I had with my marriage. He listened caringly, assured me of their full support, and asserted his confidence that when the right time comes – I will make the right decision.

When we arrived home, I noticed a car parked next to the curb in my parents' yard. A figure emerged from the passenger side while the man behind the wheel remained seated. It was Erika. After a brief pleasantry, we both agreed to meet at Palmetto Park the following day to have a talk. I watched her wave goodbye as she drove away with a stranger.

Inside the house, Mom had woken the girls up to greet me at the door. Rena was ecstatic to see me home, and Niah, who was already a year old, was talking to me non-stop even though she didn't recognize who I was. Words could not describe how grateful I was to my parents for taking care of the girls in my absence.

Later that evening, my little sister Cathy, came home to find me sitting alone on the back porch. My baby sister was now a high school senior. I couldn't believe how much she had grown; she had blossomed from an annoying little brat into a beautiful young lady. We talked about what was going on in her life and the plans she had after high school. Eventually, our conversation turned to the topic of what I had been through with Erika. She listened attentively without interruption as I ranted about the mess I was in. At the conclusion of my discourse, my sister simply asked, "Why do you feel that you have to put up with it? Why not just leave and take the girls?"

My sister made it sound so easy, and I wished it were so. A part of me wanted to do just as she said, but there was also the other side of me that insisted on staying at all costs. "I wish it was that simple, Sis. There are reasons that I can't explained as to why I stay, but one thing that I do know is that I desperately want my children to have the privilege of being raised by their real parents. And for that, I'm willing to do anything."

Tossing her hands up in the air, Cathy said, "Oh brother, being raised by your real parents is not all that great. If both of you are unhappy, your children will know it and it will surely affect them. Don't you remember the time when we sensed Mom and Dad were unhappy, it affected us? You couldn't wait to get the hell out of the house. Remember?"

Somehow, my sister's words made a profound impact on the persistent desire I had for my children. I held on to this conviction for so long, as if it was the cure for everything I thought was missing in my life. Cathy's assertion to the contrary prompted me to rethink the belief I had of how things were, instead of how I wanted them to be. She was absolutely correct that if Erika and I were living in misery, the environment we shared with our children would be just as toxic. Unbeknownst to my little sister, she had just talked some profound sense into me.

Erika and I met at the local park the following day. She came by herself this time. In broad daylight, I could readily see the strain of a turbulent year that had taken its toll on her: the dark bags under her eyes, the weight loss, and the lines on her face. I also noticed she had trouble looking me straight in the eye. Perhaps it was caused by the guilt and shame of everything that happened, or maybe it was just another side effect from her drug use.

Erika confirmed the things she had divulged in her letter; the running away, the heroin use, the prostitution, all of it. Up until that moment, a part of me was still clinging to the remote hope that the contents of her letter weren't true, that it had all been a cruel hoax to test my will power - but it was all true. It wasn't just a bad dream that I could wake up from.

For as long as I had known her, my perception of Erika was never black and white. Her ordeal as an incest victim had always tilted my views and opinions in her favor. Whenever she did something wrong, I had always looked at it from the standpoint that she was the victim, deserving of a break. Erika had counted on and exploited my kindness and generosity for so long, that even I was at a loss on where to draw the line. But on that particular day, I no longer saw Erika in different shades of grey. In a lucid moment of clarity, I saw her for who she truly was.

It was crystal clear to me that Erika was never going to change. If I chose to stay with her, one of two scenarios would likely occur - I would either completely lose my mind, or I would be pushed over the edge and land myself in prison. In either case, my daughters would suffer the consequences. It was a clear cut choice; stay with Erika and sink together, or take a chance on making it on our own. Though the possibility of the latter option may be bleak, at least it offered a glimmer of hope. At this point, hope is all I have.

I requested full custody of our girls and for Erika to walk free. I offered to take full responsibility for all the debts we had incurred, and the assurance that she'd never be required to pay for any child support. In return, I asked for her to walk away and stay out of our lives. Much to my surprise, she offered no resistance and willingly agreed to my terms.

I held out my arms for a hug goodbye, and we embraced for the last time. I felt her quivering like a frightened child and my heart sank, but I knew that this was the end. As we let go, I curiously asked, "What will you do then when you're no longer young and beautiful?"

Playfully, she replied, "Lower my price?"

We laughed awkwardly as we turned and walked away.

Letting Erika go was one of the most painful decisions I ever had to make. There were a couple of factors that weighed heavily on my decision. Walking away from my marriage went against my deeply held beliefs that were bound by cultural traditions. I had gone against the Filipino moral code of self-sacrifice, forgiveness, and to never give up, no matter the circumstances. The Filipino collectivist side of me would not hesitate to follow Erika to infinity, even if it killed me. However, the American individualist in me reasoned that to endlessly support her reckless behavior would only serve to enable her further. It was not only foolish, it was irresponsible. Enough was enough.

The other factor at play was my personal struggle with abandonment issues. My biological father had never been a part of my life, my mother had left me when I was only six, and, at fifteen, I had to sever my ties with the only family I had ever known, Grandma Rufina. I thought my marriage to Erika was going to be the solid and lasting family that I had always wanted. I fought as gallantly as humanly possible, and willing to do anything to protect my need for a sense of belonging. In the end, Erika's demons proved to be far stronger than my best defenses.

What Erica's father and uncle had done to her was unforgivable. No child should ever be subjected to such an atrocity. Their actions damaged her profoundly and created a ripple effect felt by everyone in her life. I had spent our time together trying to right the wrongs done to her. It took six years of my life only to realize that I couldn't save her from herself; the harder I tried, the more self-destructive Erika had become.

Mental health issues and substance abuse are serious matters that require professional treatment. Erika needed help, but she defiantly toughed it out on her own, falsely believing that she could self-medicate her problems away. She chose to fight her demons alone, a private battle that ripped her apart every time. Her continued refusal to seek medical attention is beyond comprehension. Perhaps she had lived with her demons for so long that she found comfort in her misery, or possibly it was her way of punishing herself, or maybe she just wanted to punish those who loved her like she had been made to suffer by those she loved and trusted. Whatever her reasons may have been, at that point, I no longer cared. I had reached my limit and that was as far as I was willing to go.

My next duty station was Fort Bragg, North Carolina, the home of the airborne division. I was likely to be engaged in frequent field training exercises and have to deploy on short notice. It was not the ideal environment for a single parent to raise two young daughters in, so I arranged for my girls to stay with my parents while I finished my last two years of military duty.

CHAPTER 8

BEYOND THE LIMITS OF FEAR

"Fear kills more dreams than failure ever will."

- Suzy Kassem

***

It took ten long years for me to reach a point where I felt comfortable articulating my thoughts in English. The improvement made me feel empowered, though I continued to struggle with many unfamiliar words, grammatical details, and my thick accent. At twenty five, I spoke just enough English to be confidently dangerous. I somehow went through a crazy phase of incessantly wanting to impress people with my developing linguistic skills. I would memorize movie lines and song lyrics that sounded profound to me, though in most cases, I couldn't grasp what these lines meant. I'd practice enunciating the words properly, and when the opportunity presented itself, I'd slip them in a casual conversation to show off my mastery of the English language.

On one occasion, I found myself uttering these words: "The actual message that reached the eyes may be quite different by the way the feature is ultimately perceived, which is to say that looks can be deceiving."

In response, the person behind the counter politely asked, "Does that mean you want the supersize meal, sir?"

Another crazy example was when I blurted out a quote from my rock star idol, David Lee Roth. "Man has two basic instincts that are primarily responsible for his continuous existence, and that is the drive to survive and the necessity to procreate the race."

I concluded by saying, "Having said that, I'd like to have two tacos, a burrito, and a small Coke."

My daughter Rena was the catalyst who eventually weaned me off of this strange compulsion. She brought me to the realization that regurgitating some amusing lines did not change the fact that I didn't really know much of anything. The limited worldly knowledge I had was tested and exposed by my oldest daughter.

I spent a month long vacation in California before moving on to North Carolina. I often drove the girls to our favorite spot in Laguna Beach, where they kept each other occupied playing in the sun all day. On our way home one day, Rena, who was only five at the time, took notice of the small blue reflectors mounted in the middle of the street. Curiously, she asked what they were for. I didn't have a clue what they were, but I didn't want to appear like an idiot in front of my children. I tried to buy some time as I scrambled in my head to make up an answer. We passed by several more of these blue reflectors, as she repeatedly pointed them out to me. Another minute had gone by when I finally responded, "It's a flood marker, baby. When the road is flooded, that's how the drivers can tell where the middle of the road is located."

She paused for a moment and said, "But Daddy, they're very tiny. How could anyone see them under water?"

Naturally, my next logical step was to cover up a lie with another lie. "Good question, Rena. You see, when the blue marker is underwater, it's designed to light up so people will know not to drive over the opposite side of the lane."

Little did I know that my answer would only open up a Pandora's Box of never-ending "what if" scenarios: What if the water is muddy? What if its tiny battery dies? What if it gets run over by a car, will it come off? And so on. My child would not stop with her relentless grilling. It had gotten to a point that when her interrogation was finally over; I wished I hadn't lied to her in the first place.

Soon after, I learned through my friend Matt Smerber, a fireman, that the blue marker on the street was, in fact, a fire hydrant indicator. Each blue marker is paired with a fire hydrant parallel to it on the curb. According to Matt, such a device provides a convenient way for firemen to spot the hydrant's location from a distance as they approach the scene of an emergency.

My daughter had asked a relatively simple question that I didn't know the answer to. It made obvious the scores of troubles that can easily be avoided just by admitting to not know the answer. It got me thinking, *What would I do then when my daughters grew up and asked the real tough questions: How does the economy work, what role does politics play in our society, or what career choice should they make?*

Children naturally look up to their parents for answers and they take every word as the absolute truth. It's an awesome responsibility that I felt inadequately prepared for. After the incident with Rena, there was no way that I would think on the fly again and provide them with made-up answers. The possibility of my daughters discovering my ignorance prompted me to seriously assess my educational level. The thought of actually going to college seemed like a monumental task; no one on my mother's side of the family had ever finished high school, much less gone to college. But the craving to do something about the gravity of my lack of formal education, trumped even the worse of my fears and self-doubts. It was a drive that prompted me to consider the possibility of going back to school.

I also realized that at this point in my life, I had never been in a better position to pursue such an ambitious goal. For one thing, I no longer had Erika to answer to, and most importantly, my comprehension of the English language had vastly improved; a progress that was a game changer. It was an amazing experience, for example, to actually understand the dialogue in movies, or be able to read books, or articles in newspapers and magazines, allowing me to peer into worlds outside of my own.

The years I had spent living in the shadow of ignorance created an unquenchable thirst for knowledge. Breaking through the language barrier ignited my passion to discover more of the world around me. There were so many questions I wanted to ask and so many things I wanted to learn. For example, I wanted to know about the vital role politics, philosophy, psychology, economics, and science play in my day to day life. For so long, these ideas were far beyond my reach, and now they were at my fingertips. The lure of endless possibility gave me the hope and belief that anything was possible.

It was during the latter part of my stay in California, at twenty four, when I read my first book from cover to cover. After Erika and I separated, I worried obsessively and had difficulty sleeping at night. The possibility of the painful experiences of the past repeating in the future, and the fear of what tomorrow may bring, vexed me. I would agonize about the past and the future a year in advance, all the while completely neglecting the present. My mind constantly churned negative thoughts; it came and went as it pleased. My thoughts had complete control over me instead of the other way around. I didn't know how to stop the constant chattering of my mind.

Out of sheer desperation, I ventured into a book store one afternoon and wandered into the self-help section. I looked through the numerous selections on the shelf, and one particular book stood out because of its corny title that made me chuckle. **You Are the World** written by J. Krishnamurti.

I pulled out the skinny paperback tightly squeezed between other competing "how to" books on the shelf, and curiously scanned through it. The gist of what I read was, *How you feel inwardly is projected outwardly, and that constitutes the world, so therefore, you are the world.*

I found the concept interesting and wondered if I was projecting the whirlwind of chaos going-on inside my head. Out of curiosity, I ended up purchasing the book that would profoundly change my life. I was so engrossed by its content from the moment I opened the pages that I read the entire book in less than a week. This inconspicuous work of J. Khrisnamurti, enabled me to take full control of my thoughts, breaking its long strangle-hold over me. Silencing thoughts' endless negative chatters was the peace of mind I so desperately needed. And this unassuming little book, delivered.

I arrived in Fayetteville, North Carolina's humid subtropical climate on July 8th, 1985. Like so many times before, whenever I first arrived at my new assignment, I'm always greeted with gloomy weather, and Fort Bragg was no exception. The dreary weather seemed to reflect the feeling of emptiness I felt being a lone stranger in an unfamiliar environment. Times like these heighten the senses, providing the unfamiliar a fresh perspective, devoid of labels, judgments or opinions. Seeing things as is also brings the glaring reality of my being utterly alone - moments that always make me long for loved ones I left behind.

It was in Fayetteville that my passion for higher learning rooted and flourished. I had arrived with a new sense of hope and aspiration to reach for something much larger than what my wildest imagination could conceive. Graduating from college was definitely in my mind's eye. However, getting past the tight grip of my own insecurities posed a real challenge. The harsh critic in me, fearful of change, readily tried to convince me as to why such an ambitious goal was a complete waste of time: I never did well academically, it's too late to go back to school, and I'd be the oldest person in class. These negative thoughts did bother me at first, but not long enough to squelch the burning desire I had for higher learning. It was a need that I simply could not ignore, a yearning that was larger than my worse fear.

Since I didn't have a mentor to lean on for advice and motivation, I had to make do with what's available and opted for the next best thing, reading. Despite the fact that I was, and still am, a slow reader, I began to expand my reading habits to a large extent. I wanted to find inspiration and encouragement to take the big leap. I read biographies of remarkable men and women, and articles in magazines and newspapers about individuals who have risen above their personal obstacles and limitations of their circumstances. After reading piles of these inspiring stories, I noticed a thread of commonality shared by these extraordinary individuals - their great appreciation for higher learning: from Martin Luther King, to Douglas MacArthur, to Bruce Lee.

It was an observation that compelled me to summon all the courage I had and walk myself to the Registrar's Office. On my way there, I assured myself that school would be different this time around; classes are conducted in a language that I could, now, finally understand. I ignored my nagging fear, knocked on the door, and signed up for my first college level course, Basic Algebra.

I was twenty six when I crossed the line into the academic unknown. Asians are stereotyped as naturally gifted in Math and Kung Fu. I don't know what happened to me because I really sucked at both. Having been only exposed to basic arithmetic, Algebra turned out to be a nightmare course for me. I did persevere and managed to get a "B" for the semester. Passing a class I wasn't so good at, boosted my confidence. On the next semester, I registered for another evening course, American History; a class I thoroughly enjoyed and did very well. These small steps helped form the belief that, indeed, it's possible for someone like me to earn a college degree. I can do this.

As the remaining year of my military contract drew near, I had to rethink the reality of my financial situation. I was still deep in debt, had two young daughters to support, and couldn't afford not to have a steady income. As re-enlistment incentives, the Army offered to send me to college for six months, in full time status, and tuition free. After careful consideration and sound advice from my parents, I re-enlisted for another three. The short-term goals I had in mind were to pay off all my debts and acquire my Associate's Degree.

For the ensuing six months, I was a full time student at Methodist College, a private university in Fayetteville. I took full advantage of the opportunity and crammed-in as many general courses I could comfortably handle. I was living a dream.

It was in that picturesque college campus where I learned about the great role the African-American civic leaders had played during the Civil Rights Movement. I learned how they bravely crossed the boundaries of injustice, challenged the prevailing system, and dared to demand equality and liberty for all. Night and day, they marched along city streets by the thousands, and fearlessly took the brunt of the brutal consequences that followed. Many of them have paid the ultimate sacrifice for the cause during those turbulent years. I was in awe by their willingness and tenacity to fight a battle that seemed insurmountable. They fought for and won the rights and privileges that benefited all minorities in today's America. As a member of the minority group, I was humbled and grateful by the bravery of these men and women who made it all possible for me and my children.

It was also in Fayetteville, outside the class room's safe boundary, where I learned an important truth – an encounter with raw prejudice. Growing up in the Philippines, I viewed the United States of America through rose-colored glasses. For as long as I could recall, Filipinos had always thought of themselves as America's favorite people.

I remember heroic tales of bravery by American soldiers who valiantly fought against the Japanese Imperial Army during World War II. Scenes of fighter planes dog fighting high above the clouds, showcasing the American dominance in the sky. These were stories that played out in my back yard told by the men in my town, war survivors, who had witnessed it all with their own eyes. *America's Favorite* was a title we proudly embraced. My American stepfather's devotion to my mother and me was a confirmation of this wonderful imagery. It was a universal truth that no one ever doubted - until the day I encountered a man from Manila.

The conversation took place in Manila during one of my many failed attempts to get to the States. I was sitting alone outside the house where Grandma and I were staying when a man in his mid-forties came over and sat next to me. He casually introduced himself and mentioned that he had heard I was about to join my parents in America. After engaging in small talk, the man said something that completely caught me off guard. In a no-nonsense tone, he said, "Just be aware that white Americans don't like people of color. Not even Filipinos."

I was so offended by his statement that I instantly blocked out everything else he said afterward. His opinion was so unconventional; it contradicted and challenged the cozy image I had of Americans. I was so disturbed by what he said that I found his mere presence, repulsive. I politely thanked him for the warning and hurriedly went inside the house to get away from him.

After living in the United States for ten years, I had not encountered anything like what the man in Manila had warned me about. The closest I had come to experiencing this type of behavior was only during those occasional cases of mistaken identity. For example, I could be standing in a hotel lobby and a guest would mistook me for a concierge and hand me his jacket. I could also be walking back to my table at a nice restaurant and a diner would flag me over to her table only to ask me to bring her check. Other than these infrequent moments of "innocent ignorance," I had never experienced an outright prejudice from white Americans. However, the experience I had in Fayetteville of having been at the receiving end of pure racism aimed directly at me, not only challenged, but shattered the cozy image I had of white Americans.

It happened one afternoon in a mall parking lot on my way to catch the six o'clock movie show with my friend Charlie. I was locking my car door when I noticed three Caucasian men, also in their mid-twenties, walking in my direction and made eye-contact with one of them as they were passing. As I slipped the keys in my pocket, I heard one of them said, "Hey, Chink!"

I wasn't sure if I heard him correctly, or if he was even talking to me. He quickly removed all my doubt when he followed through with, "Yes, I'm talking to you, Chink! What the fuck are you going to do about it?"

Judging by his slurred speech and bloodshot eyes, it was apparent to me that he had been drinking. I told him that if he couldn't handle his liquor, he shouldn't be drinking, and for him to move along. Becoming more belligerent, he dared me, "So what if I'm drunk? Come sober me up, Chink."

By then, my friend Charlie, who was also of Asian descent, was eager to pounce on this idiot. I intervened and advised Charlie not to lower himself to the agitator's level. The other two men didn't say much - it was the smallest guy who was doing the trash talking. As Charlie and I continued to make our way to the mall entrance, the three of them got in their pick-up truck and peeled past us. They drove by the mall entrance, yelling for everyone around to hear, "Chinks go home! You commies need to get the fuck out of my country! We don't want you here!"

Charlie and I went on to watch the movie as we intended, but we sat through the whole picture motionless. My eyes were fixed on the movie screen, but my mind played the humiliating incident over and over again. In the privacy of my thoughts, I tried to make sense of what had happened that afternoon. I couldn't understand why anyone, without provocation, would spew such hate filled, racist words simply because of the color of my skin. It was painful knowing that the positive image of white Americans I had held all my life had been abruptly shattered by the ignorance of these individuals.

Later that evening as I pondered the disturbing event, the man from Manila came to mind. I remembered the stern warning I had gotten from him. Perhaps his strong opinion of white Americans may have been rooted in personal experience. Only then did I realize that he hadn't spoken out of malice; he only wanted me to be aware of the unpleasant side of America that exists. On that day, I finally understood his point.

The incident caused me to re-evaluate my long held beliefs of the America that I loved. In an attempt to keep these ideals intact, I tried to make sense out of something senseless. Pondering out loud: *Didn't these people know that America was founded by immigrants, that at some point of their family history, their ancestors were immigrants like me? Did they actually believe that they could bully people of color to move out of the country? Had they ever considered how it would feel if their sons and daughters were discriminated against based on how they look?* These and many other questions momentarily preoccupied my attention, but it was an exercise in futility. No matter how hard I tried, I would never understand how a man could condemn another man simply by the color of his skin. Only an intolerant mind could make sense of bigotry.

The man from Manila may have made his point, but even still, I respectfully disagree with his wide-ranging assessment that America is generally a racist society. What I've learned that day was that, indeed, racism still exists and is very much alive, but to conclude that all Americans are racists is simply not true. It's a point of view that goes against the day-to-day experiences I've had living amongst Americans.

The despicable act of these men did not reduce me into labeling every American as racist, or tag the entire Southern region as such. I knew better. I've worked and played amongst many Southerners who were nothing like these racist men.

There was a time in American history when the dark side of humanity had its way in government, but bigotry is no longer the law of the land. The vast majority of people I've come in contact in my travel all around the globe, are generally good-natured individuals. However, every now and then, I do run into racist degenerates ruled by hate, resentment, and envy - whose only solace is to pin the blame for their own shortcomings on the voiceless outsiders. I've come across these individuals, not only in America, but in other countries as well, including the Philippines. Fortunately, in my personal experience, they are more of an exception rather than the norm.

It was also during my full-time status as student that I figured out a way to further improve my communication skill. I was studying for an exam, when it suddenly dawned on me that in order to speak English fluidly, I had to think in English. Prior to this realization, I had always formulated my thoughts in my native dialect, Visayan, and translated word for word into English when speaking. In the beginning I had to do it this way because I simply didn't know enough English words in my arsenal. The process of learning, accumulating, and adding foreign words into my memory bank took decades to accomplish. But even when my English vocabulary had expanded exponentially, I continued to carry-on the old habit of thinking in one language and translating it to another. It was a method that proved to be impractical. For one, it was too time consuming, and two, there were too many English words that couldn't be translated in my language, and vice versa. Thinking in English aided the flow and spontaneity in the delivery of my speech.

When my full-time status in school was up, I continued to pursue my goal by taking college courses in the evening. I rented an apartment outside the military compound in order to have peace and quiet for my study. My newfound freedom allowed me to pursue the things that I've always wanted. But between my grueling work schedule by day and the evening hours I've dedicated to my study, there was hardly anytime left for having fun. I'm a firm believer that a good healthy balance between work and play was necessary to avoid getting burnout. Not having enough time to socialize made me feel restless, causing me to cram as many activities in a small span of time. Perhaps another contributing factor to my restlessness was a subconscious desire to make up for the time I had lost for marrying at such a young age. Now that I am free, I'm learning that, like everything else in life, freedom also has its down side - its susceptibility to loneliness and boredom.

In retrospect, the manner in which I tried to fill these voids was outright reckless. The dating scene can be a perilous trip to navigate, and I certainly had my share of unwise choices that put myself in harm's way on a couple of occasions. I eventually learned that the secret to a long life is to try not to shorten it; dating a woman with a husband or boyfriend can exponentially shorten one's life span. However, what I'd yet to learn was to also avoid the other type of woman who is equally harmful, the unattainable kind.

Her name was Katherine, a school teacher who had gone to the club, where we met, to celebrate her colleague's birthday. I just knew from the moment I saw her that there was nothing that could prevent me from having her in my life. She spoke to me before a single word was even uttered between us.

A month later, I found myself sitting across the table at a nice restaurant with the woman of my dreams, who happened to be Jewish. Katherine was down to earth, refined, and appreciated honesty, but for some odd reason, perhaps out of my own insecurity, I felt compelled to take the extra steps to really impress her by appearing cleverer than I really was. I sensed an opportunity to show off when our waiter came and greeted us in a thick, French accent, I returned his greeting with the handful of French words I knew. *"Bonsoir, Monsieur, comment allez vous?"*

The waiter's eyes lit up with excitement at the prospect of speaking to me in French. As he handed us our menu, he rattled off some long winded sentences in French and concluded with what sounded like a question. He paused and eagerly waited for my response, as did Katherine.

Whatever he had said sounded poetic, but I hadn't understood a word of it. Once again, I had put myself in a position of having bit off much more than I could chew. I was mortified at the possibility of making a bad impression on our first date.

I took a deep breath and laid the menu aside and said to the waiter, *"Je ne parle pas Francais, je veux seulement impressionner les femmes. S'il vous plait, ne lui dites pas."*

As I delivered my response, I vocalized each syllable as eloquently as I could, coupling them with an array of hand gestures to convey the importance and sincerity of my words. When I finished my short French recital, the waiter stood stoned faced for a moment before finally saying, *"Ahh... Oui, Monsieur!"*

I raised my hand to give him a high five. He smiled and complied. "I shall return shortly to take your order, sir."

Katherine was impressed. "Wow! I had no idea that you could speak French fluently."

With feigned humility, I said, "I don't like to brag, but yeah... it's really no big deal."

In reality, though, what I had said to the waiter was, "I really don't speak French, I'm just trying to impress my date. Please don't tell her."

Fortunately, the waiter had understood my broken French and generously played along.

As we dined, I marveled at the candles' soft golden glow, glistening across the contours of her face; she was a perfect combination of beauty and elegance. Katherine had a natural curiosity about everything and possessed an endearing quality of putting people at ease. When we speak, she made me feel like I was the center of the universe. The evening was progressing splendidly, when suddenly, it took an unexpected turn.

In the middle of our meal, Katherine looked me straight in the eye and said, "Benjamin, I really like you. In fact, I like you a great deal. But... if anything is going to happen between us, it's only going to be purely physical, with no strings attached. Can you handle that?"

I nearly swallowed my fork as I thought to myself, *Wow! There must be a God.*

I felt like I was about to jump out of my skin from excitement, but I maintained my composure and replied, "Yes, we'll just take it day by day. No expectations and no demands."

"Excellent!"

And so began a journey of sheer ecstasy for me. In the course of the months that followed, I had gotten to know Katherine much more than I had ever imagined. There were evenings when we would just lie in bed and talk about everything and nothing, until the break of dawn. We were like long lost friends that had a thousand lifetimes of catching up to do. Indeed, she was my "better half" that Grandma Rufina had described in her stories; the one I'd be searching for the rest of my days. For me, the search was over, Katherine was the one.

Six months into our arrangement, I decided to test the waters and see if we could take our relationship to another level. We had dinner at my place, and after I finished my first glass of wine, I asked, "So, how do you feel about our arrangement, Katherine?"

Peeking over her wine glass, she said, "Actually, it's working out far better than I had anticipated."

I was pleased with her response, so I continued, "Are you ready to take it to the next level?"

She paused and glanced at me suspiciously. "What do you mean?"

I coolly replied, "I mean, I just want to spend more time with you and be able to express what I feel for you."

Katherine gently placed her wine glass on the table, crossed her arms, and leaned back in her chair, "Remember our first date, Benjamin? We made an agreement."

I said, "Katherine, that was six months ago. Back then, we didn't know each other very well. Now, we have history together."

She insisted, "That's beside the point, we had an agreement and I want to keep it that way."

What I had hoped would be another promising evening had instead brought chilling reality that this was the farthest our relationship would ever be. The more I tried to reason, the more pushback I got from her. I was crushed, and it showed - I couldn't hide my disappointment.

In the ensuing weeks, I tried over and over to change her mind, but she steadily rebuffed my appeals. I attempted to hang on for as long as I could with our arrangement, but it grew more excruciating by the day. The truth of the matter was that I loved her, and I wanted more than she was willing to give.

Seven months into our relationship, over breakfast, I informed Katherine of my intention to move on. I loved her too much to settle for anything less. In response, she simply asked, "Are you sure?"

"Yes, I am," I said.

She let out a deep sigh. "As you wish."

The mood at the breakfast table quickly cooled. The remaining conversation revolved around our separate agendas for the day, with no mention of what was to follow or if we could salvage what we had. I suppose we both knew that the break up was for the best. When we finished having breakfast, she gathered all her belongings and I walked Katherine to the door. We hugged and said goodbye, and never saw her again.

I wanted her more than anything, but in all fairness, Katherine had always been forthcoming about our agreement. She had never led me on to believe that what we had was going to be more than what it was. She was candid about her desire to, one day, marry a Jewish man. Katherine was brutally honest, and I respected her honesty. I had tried to win her over, but it just wasn't meant to be, and I had to do what was best for me in the long run. I knew it would take some time for me to come to terms with the painful reality that life must go on without her by my side. It was very difficult, but I would eventually reach a point where I could look back and appreciate what we had for what it was.

Coincidentally, three weeks after the painful episode with Katherine, my entire battalion was deployed to the Middle East for a field training exercise called "Bright Star." It was a welcome distraction that forced me out of my solitude.

Being in the vast Jordanian desert was surreal. I could turn to any four directions and see nothing but endless stretches of sand, and not a single twig in site for as far as the eye could see. Sand storms engulfed our camps almost on a daily basis. Sand as fine as talcum powder would infiltrate the tiniest crevices, wreaking havoc on our equipment and belongings. Temperatures during the day could easily reach over 100 degrees Fahrenheit, and drop precipitously at night. At dusk, a dazzling amber-colored blaze lights up the western horizon, marking the end of day. And when the evening fell, the desert sky unveils an ocean of glittering stars; so vivid, so brilliant, and so close, it seemed as though I could touch the sky. At the break of dawn, the eastern sky slowly turns to gold welcoming the rise of a new day.

My deployment to the Middle East lasted for several weeks. It was a much needed break to help me put things back into proper perspective. Upon my return, I quickly diverted my attention to my passion for Culinary Arts. The experience I had in Korea the prior year, instantly qualified me for membership to Fort Brag's Culinary Arts team. I returned to Fort Lee, Virginia, to once again compete at the U.S. Army's annual Culinary Arts Competition. It was a privilege that would be repeated again the following year. In the two year span of my participation, I received three gold medals and a trophy for "The Best Overall Entry in The Master's Category." It was one of my proudest achievements.

Five years had gone by since Granma Rufina's passing, but I continued to carry the burden of guilt inside. What bothered me most was the uncertainty of whether or not Grandma Rufina had known just how much she meant to me. I never told her I loved her. In an attempt to alleviate my guilt, I contributed to

Grandma's favorite charity, my uncles. I helped them out with what I could, be it through money or packages of goods. I knew that the gesture would have pleased Grandma Rufina, but in the long run, no amount of charitable giving could erase the feelings of guilt I had.

The closure I had been searching for came unexpectedly, in the form of a dream I had on the eve of my 27th birthday. In it, I found myself galloping on a thoroughbred horse alongside Grandma Rufina's pony. The morning sun was rising, and we had the entire equestrian park all to ourselves. We rode our horses around an oval shaped dirt track a couple of times. At some point, Grandma pulled up next to me and suggested we give the horses a break while we had some tea.

On a terrace that overlooked the equestrian park, Grandma Rufina sat across from me on a round wooden table. She chattered away while sipping her tea, as I comfortably leaned back in my seat, marveling at how healthy she looked. I could vividly see every feature and contour on my grandmother's beautiful face, right down to the thin layer of sweat that formed on the edge of her forehead.

As I savored my tea and delightfully listened to every word Grandma said, I suddenly realized that I was in a dream. At long last, I found myself face to face with the person I had been longing to see. Fearing for the dream to evaporate in an instant, I seized the moment. I drop my cup and interjected what I desperately needed to know. "Grandma, did you know how much I love you?"

She gazed at me momentarily, a pause that seemed to last forever, then finally she replied, "I always knew."

As she uttered those words to me, the dream started to fade away. I reached to hold her hand, but like the morning mist, the dream quickly vanished.

When I awoke, the bundle of guilt I carried with me for so long had been lifted. Although it was only a dream, the connection felt real. Only then was I convinced that, without a doubt, Grandma knew how much she meant to me. It was the best birthday present I ever had.

Grandma's passing taught me at an early age just how fragile life really is. The reality, that in a blink of an eye, everything near and dear to us can be taken away. The devastating loss compelled me never to take my loved ones for granted, and not let a moment slip by without saying the things I intended to say. I learned the hard way that time waits for no one.

My two years stay in Fayetteville provided the much needed time and freedom to rediscover myself. It's where I found the courage to leap beyond the boundaries of my fears and insecurities, and learned to channel my energy to achieve the things I thought was out of reach. I still have ways to go, but now I know – anything is possible.

I received my final orders from the military in the fall of 1987. I've been reassigned to the 44th Artillery Division in Babenhausen, West Germany. Ironically, Germany would have been my first duty assignment eight years earlier, if I hadn't confused Maryland for a European country. As fate would have it, I ended-up doing my last tour of duty in Europe; a place, as I had learned in textbooks, rich in history and whose influence could be traced all around the world.

CHAPTER 9

KNOWLEDGE IS POWER

"I am not bound to win, but I am bound to be true. I am not bound to succeed, but I am bound to live by the light that I have."

- Abraham Lincoln

***

In true form, my arrival at the Army post in Germany was met with gloomy weather that adequately reflected the gut-wrenching void I always felt when moving to a new location. The timing of my arrival, however, couldn't have been any better; it so happened that the barracks housing was completely full which qualified me for off-post housing at the government's expense. I always preferred to live out in the local community to get a true sense, feel, and character of the town and its citizens.

Within days, I found an apartment that was inside the compound of an old castle in the city of Aschaffenburg, just ten miles away from the military base. This magnificent place was situated right on the banks of the mighty River Main. Adjacent to it was another palace, though smaller, that prominently perched on top of a hill. The castles were linked by an astonishingly manicured botanical garden, where I imagined the royal families must have taken their many leisurely strolls from long ago. My new residence was truly an amazing place and one that I looked forward coming home to, each day.

My work schedule in Europe was far more demanding than the grueling hours I had been accustomed to. Nearly half of my time in Germany was spent on field training exercises in the vast wilderness of Grafenwoerh in eastern Bavaria. These exercises would last anywhere from thirty to forty five days at a time, where we would be completely cut-off from the outside world during the entire duration. The winter months were excruciatingly difficult, with snow piled up waist high.

During training, my battalion would break up into eleven different sub-groups; some would have as many as fifty soldiers, and others as little as ten. These individual units would then disperse in all directions throughout the immense forest, engaging in war games and firing artillery rounds. My job was to make sure that every soldier in my regiment gets, at least, two hot meals per day; breakfast and dinner. For lunch, soldiers are issued a packet of "Meals Ready to Eat," also known as MRE.

The most challenging part of my responsibility was keeping up with the constantly-moving sub-units, causing the designated pick-up point to change daily. For my troops to be on schedule for breakfast drop off at 4 a.m., meal preparation had to begin at 11 p.m. the night before. The ever-changing designated pick-up location was a logistical nightmare for my drivers who had to navigate their way through the forest in massive army transport vehicles in darkness. We had to operate in a war-like simulation, so the use of headlights was restricted to prevent the enemy from detecting our position. Fortunately, the troops in my team were very capable and always managed to locate the delivery point on time. In such harsh and high-pressured condition, a simple hot meal can serve as a huge morale booster for our troops.

When we did return back to the garrison after several weeks of isolation in the field, I appreciated even more the little time and freedom I had to do what I want. I was one of the few soldiers who had the rare privilege of living off base and the luxury of owning a car; a black 1983 VW Rabbit that I purchased from an officer who rotated back to the States. In my free time, I would often venture out alone and drive as far away from the military base as I possibly could. I was especially drawn to the city of Frankfurt, Germany's major financial hub, about forty miles from the base. It was there where most of my encounters with the German people had taken place. My initial impression of the locals was unpleasant. They seemed to come across as being too serious, humorless, and frustrated, but I was confident that it was only a matter of time when I'd eventually make friends.

December rolled in, and it was time once again for my annual pilgrimage back to my family in California. The local travel agent was very accommodating and gladly provided me with two flight options to choose from. The first was scheduled to take off from Frankfurt, a brief stop in London, then on to New York City with a nine hour layover, before a continuing direct flight to Los Angeles. The second option was a much shorter flight with only one short stop to Chicago from Frankfurt, and then straight to Los Angeles.

Initially, I was leaning towards taking the first option because of the long layover in New York City. Up until then, I had never been to New York, and nine hours break was plenty of time to take a bus to Manhattan and have a quick tour of the marvelous city. New York, NY was one of those fabulous destinations I had on my bucket list. It was very tempting.

However, when I was stationed in Korea, three years prior, I had flown back and forth from the U.S. to Asia six times, in a span of a year. At eighteen to twenty hours per flight, I had burnt myself out on flying. The thought of another long trip made my stomach turn. For this reason, and this reason alone, I chose the shorter flight via Chicago.

As it turned out, Pan-Am flight 103 to New York that I had declined; blew up in midair. A terrorist bomb had been smuggled on board, and it detonated as the plane flew over Lockerbie, Scotland. Everyone on board perished.

I was fortunate that the choice I made from what seemed like two harmless options, worked out in my favor. I would have never thought that those long, boring, and uncomfortable flights I endured three years earlier would eventually save my life. The holiday celebration with my family that year was especially gratifying, knowing that I had only been one option away from tragedy. It was yet another reminder of how everything can quickly slip away, and not take a moment for granted.

The tail end of my reenlistment was, once again, fast approaching. Although I still had a year left in the Army, the pressure to make a decision on my next career move was already mounting in me. I had reached a point in my military profession where I did not feel challenged anymore and my interest waning. I only knew that it was time for me to get out, but didn't exactly know what to pursue next. The lack of plan and the uncertainty, made the prospect of leaving the position I no longer wanted, daunting.

I grappled with this dilemma even while on vacation. On one occasion, I found myself tossing and turning, unable to get a wink of sleep thinking about the same quandary. After a few hours of restlessness, I rolled out of bed and decided to drive down to a nearby diner. I figured the fresh air would do me some good and help clear my head. As I slipped on my leather jacket and grabbed Dad's car keys on the kitchen counter, I caught a glance at a newspaper lying next to it. The headline read, "$94 Million Lotto Winner Remains At Large."

Laid beside the paper was what appeared to be a lotto ticket. Out of curiosity, I compared the numbers on the ticket with the winning numbers in the paper. To my astonishment, the numbers matched perfectly. I double-checked, triple-checked, and checked again, again, and again. Lo and behold, I held in my hand the winning lotto ticket. I nearly stumbled as I frantically searched for a pen to endorse the back of the ticket to seal the deal. Greed had taken over me. I hadn't a clue who the ticket belonged to, nor did I care to know. All that mattered at that point was that my signature was on the winning ticket.

With adrenalin pumping wildly through my veins, I felt the need to get some fresh air to calm myself down. It was still dark and chilly outside when I set-out to proceed as initially planned. The drive on my way to the restaurant was surreal; my mind struggled to come to grips with this sudden turn of events. The sheer power of what an enormous amount of wealth can acquire gives the mind a whole different perspective on everything. Moments ago, I had been struggling to figure out what to do with my future, and suddenly, I was an instant multi-millionaire.

I shook my head in disbelief of my new found fortune as the car rolled to a halt at a traffic light. While waiting for the red light to turn green, I glanced at the driver to the lane next to me. It was a Latino man well in his fifties, his weather beaten skin made me think he must be a manual laborer, who was probably on his way to work. Judging by how tired, weary, and sleepy he looked, I imagined he probably would have preferred to stay home with his wife instead of having to get up so early on this cold winter morning. He struck me as a hardworking man doing the best he can to earn a living, in the only manner he possibly can. It also hit me that even if he worked himself down to the bone, non-stop, for the rest of his life, his earnings could never come close to the kind of wealth that I now have - and the thought of it made me sad.

I arrived at the restaurant only to encounter more of the weary faces of ordinary people. I felt compelled to smile and greet everyone I came across, thinking it was the least I could do to brighten their day. I wasn't sure what prompted me to act the way I did; perhaps I was still in a state of shock.

As I sat at the counter with a cup of coffee in hand, several concerns raced through my head: What would my wealth do to my daughters? Would it spoil them, never knowing the pride of earning ones keep? What about my soon to be ex-wife, would she wage an ugly court battle to take a bigger cut of my winning? Would my friends act differently towards me?

I was pre-occupied with concerns of what could happen to my family once the news of my winning is made public. Hours later into my paranoia, I hadn't noticed that the sun had already been up for some time when I finally left the restaurant. The several cups of coffee I had were kicking in, keeping me wide awake. To kill some time, I drove down to the nearby community college; being in an academic setting made me feel at ease.

As I strolled around the campus, I couldn't help but notice that my insight on material things had drastically changed. Worldly possessions that used to appeal to my sense of pleasure didn't seem to matter much anymore. Owning a brand new sports car, for example, offered not much of a thrill, now that I could afford to buy a whole fleet of them. Even the lure of home ownership wasn't as exciting to me anymore now that I can have any property I want.

The concern that consumed me most was the uncertainty of not knowing if people would like me for who I was, and not for what my wealth could do for them. What became abundantly clear to me was that before my newfound wealth, when I was just another nobody, I knew with absolute certainty that the friends I made along the way wanted me for who I was. Strangely, there's a sense of security and comfort in knowing that, something that I hadn't even take notice of before. I spent the rest of the day in a state of bewilderment over how differently I now viewed the world as a multi-millionaire.

I found myself tossing and turning once again the following evening, still unable to get a wink of sleep. I decided to make better use of time by doing a little research on the procedure of claiming lotto winnings, and drove to a nearby 7-11 where lotto tickets are sold. The clerk behind the counter was very accommodating to my inquiries and enthusiastically explained the procedural technicalities of lotto winnings. During the course of his lengthy explanation, a stack of lotto tickets that were prominently displayed on the counter top caught my attention. They were similar to the ticket I had. Curiously, I asked the clerk what these tickets were. He explained that they were copies of the previous week's winning numbers for customers to take home and use as reference.

I had never purchased a lotto ticket in my life, so I had no clue what the difference was between the ticket I had and a real lotto ticket. As it turned out, I had been carrying a ticket that was void all along. For the last twenty-four hours, I had walked around completely convinced that I was a multi-millionaire. My illusion of grandeur evaporated just as quickly as it appeared.

Surprisingly, I didn't fall apart; in fact, I felt a tremendous sense of relief, as though a huge burden had been lifted off my shoulders. Aside from the jolt of paranoia, there was also an attachment of shame in knowing that I had taken something that I knew did not rightfully belong to me. It was only after the confusion had cleared and my feet were back on the ground that I was finally able to get some peaceful sleep. The only disappointment I felt was in knowing I still didn't have the means to complete my ambition for higher learning. For the time being, that goal remained as elusive to me as winning the lotto.

After the holiday break, I was on my way back to Germany to serve out my final year in the U.S. Army. Still unsure of what to do next with my life, I started having doubts again about the feasibility of a lucrative career outside the military. I worried that, perhaps, my wishful little goal was far too high, and thought that people like me, might be better off just serving my twenty years in the military and retire.

I was so preoccupied with these thoughts during my return flight to Europe that I hardly noticed the soft spoken lady who was seated next to me. Well into her seventies, Elizabeth had a melancholy demeanor about her. She was on her way to visit her only daughter who lived in Germany. I had always appreciated and considered it a great privilege to be in the company of seniors. I held the view that if there was anyone qualified to render any viable advice about what mattered most in life, it was the seniors, for only they had lived through and experienced life's varying stages.

Whenever an opportunity presents itself, I'd always make it a point to inquire and learn as much as I could from whatever wisdom seniors cared to impart. The question I'd often ask to get the conversation rolling would be, "If given the chance to do your past over again, would you change anything?"

The most frequent feedback I'd get revolved around regrets of never getting around to doing something they'd thought was worthwhile. The pursuit of a college education was always top of the list. I expected Elizabeth to express this common thought, perhaps because I sought words of encouragement for my personal goal. Instead, her response completely caught me off guard when she uttered. "I'd be true to myself."

After a pause, Elizabeth revealed that for as long as she could recall, she had always been attracted to women. The feeling never left her, no matter how hard she fought it. Throughout her life, she never acted on the burning secret she kept hidden inside. At the current juncture of her life, she probably never will.

Elizabeth was a product of her generation and had always done what was expected of her; she married a man, raised a family, and remained devoted to her husband until his passing four years prior to my meeting her. Despite the conflicting desire inside her, society's expectations had always been the solid obstacle in Elizabeth's life that ultimately proved to be insurmountable. Somberly, she muttered, "I just didn't have the courage to come out. I'll probably spend the rest my days wondering how things might have been."

In my case, the only real obstacle that stood in my way was me. My disadvantaged background may have been a hinder to my dreams, but that's all they were - a hindrance. At the end of the day, I only had myself to answer to. A life full or regrets was not an option, and I wasn't about to get in the way of my goals. Elizabeth's heartfelt confession stayed with me as I went on to conclude my service in the military.

The awareness of the limited time I had left in Germany, motivated me to make good use of the remaining time I had. Like a child in a candy store, I travelled to my favorite place, Frankfurt, as often as I could. My eagerness to explore prompted me to venture out even at times when it was impractical to do so. One such occasion was when I went out to a night club against the sound advice of my boss.

The First Sergeant and I had planned a midweek trip to Frankfurt to checkout a popular nightclub called the Funkadelic. The weather that day was not very agreeable; rainy, thunderous, with sweeping winds. Late in the afternoon, I received a call from the First Sergeant to tip me off that there will be a surprise "Red Alert" training exercise at 4 a.m. the next day. He warned that the entire base would be on lock down and our company would play a key role in this training exercise. He sternly advised me to remain at home and get plenty of rest, cautioning that the following day's event would require every ounce of my energy. Needless to say, our plan for the evening had been postponed.

Any reasonable person would have taken heed of this sound advice. Instead, I did a quick calculation in my head. *If I leave at 6 p.m., arriving at The Funkadelic at 7 p.m., stay for a drink or two, be out of there at 10 o'clock, home by 11 p.m., and get four or five hours of sleep - I'll be good to go.*

The computation made sense to me, so I wasted no time, and headed off to Frankfurt in the middle of a thunder storm.

As planned, I arrived at The Funkadelic at 7 p.m. and positioned myself at the bar, contentedly enjoying a cold cocktail, watching the pretty ladies go by. An hour or so into the evening, in comes a woman that caught my eye. I noticed her right away as she entered the bar and casually hung her overcoat on a hook by door. She captured my attention because of her uncanny resemblance to the young Princess Stephanie of Monaco.

As luck would have it, she sat a few empty seats away from me at the bar. Motivated by time constraints, I quickly made my move to break the ice and said hello. She smiled receptively, and an instant chemistry ensued. Well into our conversation, she asked what I did for a living. I was in a playful mood, and said to her, "I'm a professional mole reader."

She didn't pick up on the joke, and in a serious tone, she said, "I had no idea that there was such a profession. I thought they remove moles in California."

I said, "Ouch! The thought of mole removal is like a dagger to my heart."

With a puzzled look on her face, she asked, "What exactly does a professional mole reader do?"

I said, "I read moles to predict my client's future. It's a lot like palm reading, but with 100 percent accuracy."

She extended her arm to expose the tiny mole on her forearm. "What does my mole say about my future?"

I pretended to analyze her tiny mole for a few seconds before saying, "In my industry, you have a mole that we refer to as 'Nawom.' It basically means that the prediction I'm about to tell you is inevitable; it will happen, and there's absolutely nothing that you can do to change it. Therefore, my advice to you as a professional is don't fight it, simply go with the flow."

In my dialect, the word "Nawom" actual means mole. By then, she had a bit of concern look in her eyes, "Ok, so what does my mole say?"

I held her arm to take another look, "Again, no use fighting it, just go with the flow."

I slightly shook my head for an added dramatic effect, "Mmmm... Your mole tells me that you'll be going home with me tonight."

Finally, I made her smile. "I get it, you're joking! Does that pick-up line really work for you?"

I said, "It remains to be seen."

Her name was Brigitta Hildebrant, Gitta for short. We took turns buying each other drinks as we talked and danced our way through the night. I learned that, like me, she was very close to her grandmother, whom she fondly referred to as "Ommie."

Her grandfather had passed away decades ago, and her "Ommie" never remarried. She described her relationship with her parents as similar to living on an island. I didn't quite understand what she meant by it, but I let it slide, thinking there'd be plenty of time in the future to figure it out.

Gitta fondly shared her "Ommie's" wise advice about men. "Ommie said to pay close attention to how the potential man in my life treats his mother. If he can be abusive to his own mother, he will have no problem treating other women the same."

Sound advice, indeed. I made a mental note to pass it on to my daughters someday.

Gitta was incredibly engaging and gave me her full attention throughout our conversation. I was so engrossed with her company that I lost track of time. I eventually peered down at my watch and made the horrifying discovery that it was already 5 a.m. I had completely forgotten about the 4 a.m. "Red Alert" back at the base. We exchanged phone numbers and hastily said goodbye as I dashed out of the bar.

On my way home, I scolded myself for sheer lack of discipline, which had now put me in a dire predicament. An hour later, as soon as I walked-in my apartment, the phone rang. It was Gitta; she called to see if I had made it home safely. After we hung up, the phone rang again, but this time, it was my boss yelling at the top of his lungs, "Where the hell have you been? I told you not to go out, but you did anyway!"

I acknowledged I totally screwed up and assured the First Sergeant that I'd be on my way. I was so exhausted and have had too much to drink that I just had to lie in bed and take a five minute nap before turning myself in for a well-deserved tongue-lashing from my boss. Instead, I passed out and didn't wake up until noon. By the time I got to the base at 1 p.m., everyone was still running around in their full gear, combat ready. A terrible hangover pounded my head as I struggled to drag myself out of my car.

I stood in front of the First Sergeant stone faced as he turned blood red with anger. In a classic "this is going to hurt me more than it does you" speech, he reprimanded me to remain in the barracks for a full week as punishment. He said that I reeked of alcohol, making his office smell like a brewery, and told me to get out.

A month later, the First Sergeant and I finally made our trip to Frankfurt. Gitta graciously joined us and played host, showed us around her fine city. After we dropped Gitta home at the end of the evening, my boss commented, "Now I know why you lost track of time when you met Gitta. I probably would have done the same."

Gitta was exceptional; she was well travelled, knowledgeable on a wide range of subjects, and incredibly eloquent. Like a personal advisor, she provided answers to the many questions I had about the puzzling German culture. Having her acquaintance was a privilege.

For instance, I had gotten the impression that Germans were generally ill-mannered and rude. It was an opinion formed through my numerous street encounters with the locals who had given me dirty looks for saying hello. I explained that in California, it was acceptable to greet a total stranger in the street with a smile or a simple hello.

Gitta explained that saying hello to a total stranger, though seemingly innocent, was considered disingenuous by German standards. The way the Germans saw it, *"You don't know me and I don't know you, so why pretend we do?"*

She added that such pretentious effort the Germans find insulting. I wanted to counter by asking, *How much of an effort does it really take to simply say hi and raise a smile?* But I stop myself when I realized that I was doing it again - imposing my value system on another culture.

Another grand mystery that Gitta helped solved, had to do with the great city of Ausfhart. Anywhere I ventured on the German freeway system, the autobahn, I would always see road signs pointing to the city of Ausfhart. Seeing the road sign constantly gave me the impression that Ausfhart must be another major German city, perhaps even larger than Frankfurt.

I asked Gitta if we could travel and spend the day to Ausfhart. She couldn't make out what I was saying even when I repeated it slowly, so she suggested I point out the next road sign that we came across for the city. Not long after we merged onto the Autobahn, I excitedly pointed one out. "Look! Look! There it is! Let's go there today!"

Gitta looked at me with bewilderment. "Benjie, the sign says Ausfhart... it means Exit."

There was silence at first, and then we both burst out laughing.

My association with Gitta and her circle of friends had given me real glimpse of German culture. One fascinating characteristic I observed about the German people was their natural tendency to be very analytical and think things through. In most everything Gitta did, for example, she seemed to never make a decision in haste; always eyeing the big picture and weighing the pros and cons. It's no wonder Germans make good engineers. I discovered that beneath the seemingly aloof exterior, Germans are genuine, affable people, and likely to be a friend for life.

I once asked Gitta how it felt to belong to a society that was admired around the world for its great engineering prowess, unlike my native land, which was known only for extreme poverty and political corruption. Gitta said she wished engineering was the only thing the Germans were known for, but that the world hadn't forgotten Germany's part in World War II. In her travels abroad, she'd sometimes come across individuals who made it a point to test her knowledge of the atrocities committed by the Germans during the war. She explained that it was embedded in her society to carry some degree of culpability for what had happened during her grandparents' generation. Gitta asserted that the guilt of what happened in World War II was still an inescapable part of being a German citizen, or at least in her generation.

Gitta and I dated for the entirety of my last year in Germany. In that span of time, we manage to develop and cultivate a small community of friends, comprised mostly of military officers and their wives in my battalion. The officers welcomed us without reservation, despite my status as a Non-Commissioned Officer. Sergeants and Officers normally didn't socialize when off duty.

Whenever my unit deployed for weeks-long field training exercises, Gitta and the officers' wives would put together nice packages to send to the field. The prolonged length of time away from home can dampen the spirit a bit; receiving those packages filled with homemade goodies was an awesome treat that kept me connected to the outside world.

I discovered long ago that regardless of how mesmerizing a place or spectacular a structure may be, its splendor is only half as memorable if there's no one there to share it with. Having Gitta by my side, made even the most ordinary things delightful. The time we had Germany was one of the best times of my life, and one that I wished would last a while longer. But the time for me to move on was fast approaching, and the inevitable talk between Gitta and me, loomed overhead.

One day in early fall, as we strolled along the botanical garden where I lived, Gitta casually asked, "Your military contract is about to expire. Have you thought about what you're going to do?"

The truth was that I hadn't given it much thought, even though I only had three months left in the service. Internally, I was almost certain that I'll probably end up reenlisting again. The limited alternatives I had didn't look too promising. It was a sad reality that I didn't want to admit to myself, and one I tried to avoid for as long as I could. However, with Gitta, there were no pretenses and just be forthright, "I really don't know what I'm going to do. To be perfectly honest, I'm torn. On one hand, I really feel that I owe it to myself to try to live up to my full potential. On the other hand, at thirty, I am terrified of having to start all over again, with no prospect for a decent job, having no idea what career to pursue, and children to support."

Gitta placed her hand on my back and gave it a gentle rub. "I've watched you struggle for months, and I know that you can do so much more. If this were a perfect world, devoid of fear and all the ifs and buts, what would you like to do?"

I replied, "What I want more than anything is to get out of the military and get my Bachelor's Degree."

"What stops you?" she asked.

Hesitantly, I responded, "It's the lack of funds. I am afraid I'll end up working long hours in some kitchen for minimum wage and forfeit my studies."

Gitta continued to prod. "Have you calculated how much money you'll need in order to focus on your studies without having to work?"

I said, "No, I have not since I already know that I don't have the means to obtain such an amount."

She insisted, "Just indulge me. Knowing the price tag would put things in perspective and tell you if what you're after is realistic or not."

I nodded in agreement. "Yeah, maybe you're right."

A couple of weeks later, Gitta revisited the issue. This time, I had taken her advice and come up with a lump sum figure for my college fund. We combed over an itemized list that detailed every expense in my budget plan. Gitta seemed delighted that I had taken her suggestion into serious consideration. A few weeks went by without any further discussion about my future plans.

Then one Friday afternoon, Gitta arrived at my place carrying a black briefcase. She and I planned to just stay home for the weekend. It dawned on me that she had come straight from work, and had perhaps brought some unfinished work with her to touch on over the weekend.

As soon as she entered my apartment, Gitta laid the brief case flat on the dining table, unlocked it, pushed it in my direction, and told me to take a look inside. I gazed at her in bewilderment as I pulled the case closer. Inside the briefcase were several bundles of German currency; the funds I needed to get a fresh start. And just like that, Gitta handed me my future. There was no contract or promissory note to sign; just a greeting card with a message that said, "You can do it. I believe in you."

I was speechless; words couldn't describe the gratitude I felt at that moment. In an instant, she brought to reality dreams that, until then, could only exist in my wildest imagination: a college degree and a new career. It also struck me that after being away from my family for so many years, I was finally going home for good. Gitta had made it all possible.

The Company Commander and First Sergeant tried to persuade me to reenlist when they learned of my intention to leave the military. They guaranteed my prompt promotion to Sergeant First Class, if I should choose to stay. I thanked my superiors for extending their kind offer, but politely declined. It's been a great privilege to serve alongside the soldiers in my unit. These were dedicated, tireless, hard-working men and women with whom I'd spent countless hours in the garrison and in the harsh environment of the field. They taught me the essential elements of leadership, responsibility, and commitment; values that I would carry with me for the rest of my life.

My days in the Germany were ending and it was especially difficult to break away from the small community of friends that Gitta and I had become a part of. They were family to us, and leaving them was no easy feat. I looked forward to the next chapter of my life with great anticipation, and though the military life wasn't always easy, I suspected that I'd look back at my time in the U.S. Army with fondness.

The day before my departure, I took along walk in the botanical garden in my apartment to relish its splendor for the last time. I was delighted to come upon Mr. Miller comfortably seated on our usual spot. He was an elderly man who regularly spent his afternoons on a bench along the hill side, over-looking the spectacular view of the River Main below.

Mr. Miller, of Pakistani descent, had married a German citizen, and had lived most of his life in Germany. Well into his late sixties, he spoke English eloquently which, together with his well-groomed silver beard and sharp attire, gave him the appearance of a distinguished scholarly gentleman. I first met Mr. Miller on that same exact bench shortly after I moved into my apartment two years earlier. The manner in which we met was just short of a wish come true.

It was in the middle of the week, I sat on that bench alone, wishing I had a wise friend, a confidant or mentor to lean on for advice. As I sat there deep in contemplation, from a distance, a gentleman appeared in my peripheral vision. He slowly made his way towards me, and as he reached where I sat, he stopped to ask if I would mind sharing the bench. Gladly, I scooted over and offered him a seat. After a brief introduction, Mr. Miller expressed his astonishment at seeing a young man like myself, take some time alone to enjoy a moment of self-reflection. It was a day that marked the beginning of what would become many afternoons with Mr. Miller. We've spent numerous times just basking in spectacular sunsets, while exchanging views on important, as well as trivial, matters and curiosities in our daily lives.

In what would be my final meeting with Mr. Miller, I broke the news of my departure and expressed my gratitude for having had him as a friend. He asked what I planned to do when I got back to the States. Excitedly, I laid out the details of what I intended to pursue next. Sensing my enthusiasm and eagerness for higher learning, Mr. Miller asked, "Why is a college degree so important to you, Ben?"

Admittedly, his question caught me off guard. I had known the man long enough to know that he wasn't looking for an obvious answer. I pondered a moment, and then said, "Because the more I learn, the less insecure I am about myself."

He nodded and said he was pleased that I was about to embark on a new and exciting chapter, but he also articulated his sadness in knowing I would no longer be around. We went on to spend the rest of the afternoon the way we had done many times before; consumed in our never-ending discussions about life.

As the sun slowly disappeared over the horizon, we shook hands and bid our farewells. His parting words to me were, "Ben, it's not the acquisition of knowledge that's important. What matters most is what you do with it. Be sure to apply the knowledge that you've gained."

Until then, I pursued higher learning with the notion that knowledge was inextricably intertwined with power. Mr. Miller's parting words had not only challenged my notion, but also added the missing element to the old adage I had adhered to for so long: "Knowledge is power."

I couldn't agree more with Mr. Miller's assessment that "application" was crucial in bridging the gap between "knowledge" and "power."

Only then did I come to realize that even if I gained the best knowledge money could buy, if I don't apply it, then it would remain as it was, wasted knowledge.

Therefore, the precise adage ought to be: "Applied knowledge is power."

PART—IV

CHANGED PERCEPTIONS MODIFIED ACTIONS

CHAPTER 10

FADING CULTURAL CODES

"Education is a progressive discovery of our own ignorance."

- Will Durant

***

The military's necessary culture of respect for authority, strict obedience, and strengths in teamwork, bore a striking resemblance to the collective conditioning I had in the Philippines. My ten years of service in the U.S. Army, in a way, provided a continuation and reinforcement of my long held belief in conformity. This familiarity naturally led me to believe that the larger American population held the same collective views as I did.

I integrated into the civilian society unaware that I was still very much operating under the old Filipino cultural mindset. It was during my college years and into my early climb on the corporate ladder that I would discover just how out of step my thinking was to the stride of the American way. At almost every level, my Filipino mindset of "us" frequently clashed with the American stance of "me." It was during these times when I had to seriously reexamine my core values, identify the accepted norms, learned to adapt to the new ways, and come to terms with having to let go with the old ways.

I received my honorable discharge from the U.S. Army in the early spring of 1990. While in school, I wanted to live near my parents' home to make up for the many years we'd been apart. California State University San Bernardino's proximity to Fontana was the perfect choice where I registered to begin the following fall semester. I took some time off to get settled-in and spend some time with the kids and family before taking on the monumental task of fulfilling my dream of becoming a college graduate.

The arrangement that Gitta and I had agreed on, was for me to devote the next three years to my studies, while she remained in Frankfurt. The plan was for her to spend a few months with me in California before the fall semester, then for me to occasionally fly to Germany during school breaks, and for her to spend her vacations in California with me. Gitta followed shortly after my arrival in Fontana. This was her first trip to the United States, which should have been an exciting time for both of us, but instead, it was marred by concerns regarding my daughters.

On my first day home from overseas, I was greeted with the news that a month prior to my return, Erika, had brought the Sheriff to my parents' house and demanded the children's release to her custody. I had foolishly procrastinated filing for divorce and hadn't done so at that point, which technically meant that Erika, still had rightful custody of our children. The Sheriff had no choice but to uphold her legal rights.

To make matters worse, Erika and her new fiancé had already relocated to Wisconsin with the girls. The most disturbing part of all was that they were living with Erika's father, the man who raped his own daughter. Erika's uncle, who molested her, also lived nearby. It was a nightmare waiting to happen.

It took a couple of days of heated discussions before Erika and I managed to reach a compromise. She agreed to return the girls to California until she and her fiancé could settle down and have a place of their own, far away from her father's and uncle's reach. In return, we agreed that when she was well situated on her end, the girls would live with her during school year and I would have them during their summer vacation. The final point in our new agreement was the reversal of our custody roles once I graduated from college.

With concessions reached from both sides, Erika had the girls flown back to California within days. They arrived just a few days after Gitta did. My oldest daughter Rena was already nine, and Niah had just turned six. Gitta and the girls bonded instantly; she adored them and they revered her.

We took the girls for a long-overdue vacation in Hawaii. We stayed with my sister Gina, who had gotten married and moved to the island of Oahu with her husband and two daughters; Jackie and Ashley. My nieces were slightly younger than my daughters, and they instantly kept each other occupied. Gitta and I took the four girls with us all around the island. We spent most of our days looking for new spots to explore, be it hiking trails, waterfalls, or an endless day on the beach. For the girls, the day was never complete without stopping by their favorite fast food restaurant for Happy Meals.

The Hawaiian Islands reminded me so much of the Philippines, it made me feel nostalgic. So much so, in fact, that it prompted me to talk Gitta into taking a short trip with me to visit my home away from home. Gitta agreed, and my sister gladly took care of the girls during the two weeks that we were gone. It has been fifteen years since I've been gone, and the prospect of reuniting with my friends and relatives in Alumnos, thrilled me. Gitta had never been around abject poverty up-close, coupled with intense tropical heat and humidity; I was a bit concerned if she could handle it.

 When we arrived, everyone I introduced her to, welcomed her openly. The children were specially fascinated by her light brown hair, hazel eyes, and fair skin; their smiling little faces followed her everywhere. Gitta was taken aback by just how hopeless and chaotic Alumnos seemed, but was also touched by the people's warmth and friendliness. She was very supportive of my wanting to spend time with friends and relatives I hadn't seen in years, though I could tell she was outside of her comfort zone. In retrospect, however, I should have been more sensitive to how she might have felt being so out of her element. I could have offered some relief from the culture shock by taking her to a nice resort and showed her the pleasant side of the Philippines, but ultimately, I didn't.

I was too consumed with the insatiable curiosity to learn more about Grandma Rufina's final days. Perhaps, I wanted to hear that what she endured under Antastacio's care was far more tolerable than I had imagined. Instead, I uncovered the opposite of what I needed to hear from several accounts told by relatives and neighbors. According to an account by a relative, over the years my grandmother's health had steadily deteriorated to a point where it was difficult for her to physically get-out of bed. Ironically, instead of caring for his ailing mother, Anastacio's demands only grew stronger and his cruelty intensified.

On one occasion, a neighbor described how Anastacio terrorized Grandma out of bed by slitting a cat's throat in front of her and threatened to do the same to her if she did not get her "pathetic self" out of bed. These horrific stories about my uncle did not surprise me at all. I knew full well what this man was capable of. Grandma Rufina had endured Anastacio's brutality for so long that her nerves eventually gave in; often having nervous breakdowns that lead to her demise. I couldn't help but imagine how afraid and alone she must have felt in her final hours. It was such a pity that she didn't live long enough to see the difference she had made in my life.

I was also looking forward to the opportunity of interacting with my uncles once again, men I revered and feared as a child. From an adult's perspective, it was Uncle Segundo's company that I enjoyed most. Unlike my other two uncles, he wasn't intimidated by my presence. He was outgoing, outspoken, and displayed great curiosity about the outside world. Many of his worldly views were well thought out, and he frequently asked open-ended questions. Uncle Segundo was well respected and admired by the people in his community. I couldn't help but wonder, if he had been born in an economically advanced society, undoubtedly, my uncle would have made worthwhile contributions to society.

On the opposite end of the spectrum, Uncle Anastacio was held in jail awaiting trial for murder. Apparently, with Grandma being gone and no one to bully at home, Anastacio had taken his rage out on the neighborhood. During his drunken tirades, he made constant threats to blow up everyone with homemade dynamite. I saw this one coming long before my departure for the United States.

The use of homemade dynamite to catch schools of fish was the preferred method for some fishermen. It was totally illegal not only because of the inherent danger it posed to the lives of the fishermen, but also the carnage it brings to the ocean's ecosystem. But some fishermen like Anastacio, chose to disobey the law and did it their way.

In order to get the maximum kill, the explosion had to occur five to seven feet below the surface before the school of fish could dash away. It requires skill of absolute precision that could yield great catch when done properly, but can also turn deadly in an instant, if done incorrectly. And I have seen its catastrophic aftermath before.

Anastacio was good at it, and he also knew how to make his own explosives. I was about ten years old the first time my uncle sent me to fetch a small bag of explosive powder from a neighbor. He would also send me off to gather other materials, such as empty 16 ounce Coke bottles, fine pebbles, and sand. I'd be in the room with him, serving as his personal assistant when he put together what amounted to homemade dynamite.

He would walk me through every step; filling a third of the Coke bottles with fine pebbles; it served to weigh down the bottle, sinking it faster. Next, he'd pour the explosive powder to take-up another third of the bottle, topping off the remaining space with sand. A twelve inch fuse was inserted all the way down to the base, leaving a portion of the fuse protruding for detonation. To keep everything in place, the top was then sealed with a melted wax-like substance. He typically made three or four of these homemade dynamite bombs at a time.

I remember when, at the stroke of midnight on a New Year's Eve, he detonated a couple of these homemade bombs on the shoreline. Anastacio timed it so perfectly for the explosion to go off right before the bomb could reach the ocean floor, muffling the sound of the blasts and prevented the flying debris from scattering. He ignited the second dynamite with the same precision, resulting in another spectacular but unnerving sight. He later said to me, that it was his way of celebrating the New Year. But the impression that I got, was he wanted to publically demonstrate his power to annihilate. There was no doubt in my mind, the neighborhood received the same message, loud and clear.

After I left for the States, I heard stories of my uncle yelling at the neighborhood with dynamite in hand, daring anyone to challenge him. Anastacio eventually stabbed a young man to death, an 18 year old neighbor, who had the misfortune of crossing my uncle's path during his drunken rampage. I felt so bad for the victim's family that I volunteered to pay the debt they'd incurred from funeral expenses, and apologized on behalf of my family.

The pressing urge I had to come face to face with my nemesis prompted my decision to visit Anastacio in jail. This was the man who had planted fear in me and taught me how to hate. I wanted to confront my childhood monster and unleashed the wrath I carried for so long, and pass it to its rightful owner.

Up until then, I had never been to any prison facility. I pictured myself talking to Anastacio over the phone sitting behind a glass window, like I had seen in movies. But the real Philippine prison I visited was so chaotic, it was shocking. The prisoner housing structure resembled an abandoned industrial warehouse. The approximately 10,000 square feet of space were divided into three open sections. Prisoners put together their own makeshift beds and flimsy curtain walls to separate themselves from other detainees. Trenches of open sewage cut across the yard, there were inmates cooking their own meals. I even saw chickens running around the premises.

Prisoners did not have an assigned cell or bunk. When new detainees checked in, the prison guard simply instructed them to find whatever space was available and handed them a piece of cardboard to lie on. This facility was their holding cell until they actually go on trial, which could drag on for months.

After a brief body search, the prison guard opened the gate and sent me in amongst the prisoners. There were no uniformed guards present. If there were, I couldn't tell them apart from the inmates. I asked around for Anastacio, describing him by identifying the type of crime he had committed. A prisoner said he knew my uncle, and that he saw him taking a bath, and volunteered to fetch him for me. I stood in a corner of the building and waited anxiously for my nemesis to emerge.

A few minutes passed, and then an old man appeared. He was drenched from head to toe, drying himself off with his worn-out t-shirt as he approached me. It was my Uncle Anastacio. Already well into his fifties, looking malnourished, and frail, I couldn't help but feel sorry for this pathetic-looking old man. His eyes lit up the moment he recognized who I was, and shook my hand firmly. I could not believe that this feeble little man was the monster I had feared in my youth.

Seeing him in his miserable condition, disarmed the years of hatred I reserved for this man. To confront him then and unleashing my anger would be like kicking a helpless man while he's down. But my sympathy was short lived the minute Anastacio opened his mouth and began to spew his usual garbage about life's entitlements he felt were rightfully his. When asked how Grandma died, he claimed to have no clue or why she was always such a nervous wreck around him. As to why he had so much hatred for Grandpa Antonio, he reasoned that it was because the old man had never wanted to take care of him. It didn't take long for me to realize that despite all the years that have gone by, my uncle hadn't changed, and probably never will.

Anastacio's "blame the world" argument was more than I could tolerate. I interjected and told him he had been the cause of my grandmother's death. I ridiculed the idea of an able grown man like himself, expecting a crippled old man to serve him. I ranted and raved to get things off my chest that I had held for so many years.

Then I suddenly realized, I might as well have been talking to a wall. The man was incorrigible; a self-absorbed sociopath, and no words or deeds could ever change him. For so long, I carried so much hatred for this man, which was detrimental, because to carry such vicious hate took so much time and energy from me. Right then and there, I made the conscious decision to cut my losses and not waste another ounce of energy on his behalf - I let my hatred go.

The two-week stay was simply not enough to catch up fifteen years of absence. It was already time for us to leave, though for me, it sure felt like we just arrived. Gitta on the other hand, was getting antsy to get back home. The heat and humidity were unbearable and beginning to have an impact on her health. On one occasion, she passed out from heat exhaustion and had to be taken to a hospital. Luckily, she recovered quickly and was able to leave the hospital on the same day.

As an added calamity to what may have seemed to Gitta as an already exhausting trip, we almost got robbed on our way out of the Philippines. We had to take a short flight from Cebu to Manila, and landed at a small airstrip just a few miles from the international airport, where we would catch our connecting flight to Hawaii.

On our way out of the terminal, a young man in security uniform asked if we needed a taxi to the international airport. I asked what the cab fare would be, and was not impressed when he told me that it would cost 99 pesos, the equivalent of five dollars. I told the young man that we would just take our chances outside the terminal and try to get a better fare. He tried to warn me that such a move could be dangerous, unwisely, I ignored his advice.

Gitta and I went out and waded our way through a long line of taxi drivers aggressively soliciting our business. A couple of drivers literally got into a fist fight over us. The more aggressive of the fighting-drivers grabbed our luggage with the help of another man and hurriedly ushered us into the backseat of his cab. Strangely, the man who had helped also climbed on board and sat in the front passenger seat. As the driver navigated out of the crowded parking lot, I noticed that there was no meter mounted on the dashboard.

The man in the passenger seat turned to us and introduced himself as our personal bodyguard. He proudly informed us that he had handcuffs and weapons in case we encountered any danger on our way to the airport. I asked why we needed security service for such a short trip, and why there was no meter on the dashboard. The man posing as security explained that we were in a very dangerous part of town and many tourists had been robbed before. Regarding the fare meter, the driver then turned to me and said, "Don't worry about the cab fare, sir. We will take good care of you because you are one of us, and by the way, your wife has beautiful green eyes."

"How much is this going to cost us, exactly?" I asked.

He smiled and said, "For you, sir, it will only be thirty-five dollars."

"What? Thirty-five dollars for such a short ride?" I protested.

The security guy interjected, "No, Sir. Its thirty-five dollars per person, it's a total of seventy dollars, which includes my security service."

I exclaimed, "Seventy dollars for a short cab ride? You've got to be kidding me!"

"No, sir, it's not a joke," he said confidently.

I snapped, "Then stop the car! We are getting out of here! Stop the car!" I called out.

Panicked, the driver cut in. "Sir, we can't stop the cab. This is a very dangerous area."

Raising my voice, I said, "No, I think we're in far more danger with you two. If there's honor among thieves, it would be far more respectable if you just nab a purse on the street than to rob unsuspecting visitors like us. Shame on you two!"

The guard reasoned, "Sir, we are not criminals. We have families to support, and everything is very expensive here."

"Then get an honest job instead of trying to rob us," I retorted. "Do you guys realize that you're contributing to the demise of the country as a whole? Businessmen who might have wanted to invest in the Philippines would run in fear because of crooks like you."

I continued to grumble and moan all the way to our destination. By the time we arrived at the international airport, the driver said to me, "Okay, sir, you don't have to pay us anything. Just give us what you think our service is worth."

I took out one hundred pesos, and handed it to the security guy. They pleaded for more, but Gitta and I grabbed our luggage and marched straight to the terminal without looking back.

We returned to Hawaii and spent another two weeks there with the girls before heading back to California. Spring and summer flew by, and by late August it was time for us all to go our separate ways. The girls took Gitta's departure very hard; all three of them cried all the way to the airport. Erika by then had relocated and gotten settled in Oklahoma with a job and an apartment close to her mother's home. As agreed upon, the girls went back to her for the school year, and I submerged myself in my studies.

Gitta and I wrote and called each other frequently, and visited her in Germany during the Christmas holiday that year. Everything seemed to be going well; however six months into our plan, I received a letter from her, expressing the difficulty she had of our separation. She articulated her willingness to leave everything behind - her work, family, and friends - just so we could be together.

In order for Gitta to gain permanent residency in the United States, it would mean marrying her. My gut feeling told me that though I loved her so, I was not ready to get married again just yet. I reflected on all of the great things Gitta had given me: the school grant, her willingness to leave her world behind, and her unwavering belief in me. I thought long and hard, but the Filipino side of me that's prone to feel a sense of obligation and indebtedness was so strong that in the final analysis, I couldn't in good conscience, turn Gitta down.

In my response to her letter, I shared the long deliberation I had before reaching my decision to have her live with me in the States. I also made it perfectly clear that I didn't want to have any more children, and for her to seriously consider the long term ramifications of being with me. My letter may have sounded harsh, but I needed to be candid with how I really felt. Gitta replied that child rearing was not a part of her long-term plans, that she loved my daughters just the same, and like me, her focus was also on her career path.

Realizing the enormous sacrifice that Gitta was about to undertake, I was concerned about how her parents must have felt, having their only daughter relocate to another country. As a good gesture, I traveled to Frankfurt to meet with her parents, to put their minds at ease, by assuring them I wouldn't let anything bad happen to their daughter.

In the year that Gitta and I had dated in Germany, I had only met her brothers, Peter and Jan, whom I was fond of. On this trip, I got to meet Gitta's mother and beloved grandmother, Omie over dinner. Her mother did not say much, probably due to her limited command of the English language, but she was very cordial.

Unfortunately, Gitta's father chose not to participate in the gathering. For whatever reason, he just flat-out refused to meet me. I pretended as if it didn't bother me, but deep inside, it hurt. I wondered how this man could be so judgmental to pass up the opportunity to meet the man his only daughter was going to marry. He made up his mind that I wasn't worth his time. I could tell by Gitta's demeanor that her father's decision bothered her, probably more than it did me. Sadly, we had no alternative but to accept her father's choice that evening.

After the gathering, Gitta's grandmother pulled me aside to say, "Please take good care of my Gitta."

I assured her that Gitta was in good hands. She smiled, and kissed me on the cheek. One year later, Omie would pass away in her sleep.

In the spring of 1991, Gitta returned to the United States. We were married on April 14th at the San Bernardino court house, witnessed by my friend Matt Smerber and his girlfriend. We spent our honeymoon on a houseboat in Lake Powell with Matt, his girlfriend, and Matt's parents, Marge and Jim. All of us slept on the houseboat's rooftop blanketed in an evening sky, so crystal clear, that moving satellites could be seen gliding slowly across the atmosphere. In the morning, the lake surface laid perfectly still without a single trace of a ripple; appearing as though a colossal mirror had been laid out on the surface of the entire lake.

Each day, we sailed from canyon to canyon in search of our own private beach. We spent the day on water sports, canyon explorations, and afternoon cocktails over spectacular sunsets. We had an amazing time, an excellent prelude to Gitta's new start in California.

Gitta was born and raised in the fast paced environment of a booming metropolis. The slow tempo of life in suburban Fontana must have been a major shift for her, but since I've known her, Gitta never showed any disdain toward what may have seemed like a scene from "The Twilight Zone."

She maintained a "can do" attitude throughout what must have been the most trying time in her life. I watched her overcome one challenge after another. Whenever she got knocked down, she'd spring right up, and keep charging. Gitta was simply unstoppable, and it looked like there was nothing she couldn't overcome. Her quest to pass her California drivers' license was a good case in point.

Frankfurters, like most people from major cities around the world, mainly relied on public transportation for their commutes. Although Gitta has had a German driver's license, she didn't have much experience behind the wheel. After several practice runs in the parking lot of an abandoned shopping center, I guided Gitta to an isolated highway to drive on a California road for the first time. She closely adhered to my instructions and reached the open highway without any incidents. As we cruised along the open road, a German shepherd suddenly bolted out of nowhere in front of us. The dog had appeared so unexpectedly that there was no time to avoid hitting it.

The impact felt like we'd struck a cow, and Gitta quickly pulled over to the side of the road. We got out to assess the damage and to see if the dog was still alive. Unfortunately, the poor thing died on the spot. No major damage was sustained by the vehicle, just a broken signal light. Understandably, Gitta was too shaken up to keep driving; I drove the rest of the way. I thought, *What bad luck. Her first outing in an open road and of all the irony she kills a dog; a German shepherd at that.*

I was convinced that after that horrific experience, Gitta would probably not want to get behind the wheel for a while. Worse yet, she might give up driving altogether. Much to my surprise, the following day, she was ready to give it another try. And not long after, she obtained her California driver's license and drove confidently.

Her next goal was to find employment. She'd been in the banking industry her entire professional career, specializing in securities trade. Understanding the employment limitations of a small suburban town, Gitta harbored no illusions about her job prospects. She interviewed for an entry-level position at a local bank and was quickly offered a position as a bank teller.

Gitta was way over qualified for the job, but she embraced it enthusiastically and never complained. She stood behind the counter like every other employee, and dealt with the inherent challenges of dealing with the public.

It was an eye-opening experience for her to learn just how different the concept of "customer service" was applied in America, in comparison to how they view it in Europe. She even got robbed at gunpoint and had to identify the suspect at the police station. The experience was daunting and undoubtedly nerve-wrecking, but Gitta was not easily discouraged.

Four months after securing her first job, Gitta was able to obtain a better employment at an international bank in downtown Los Angeles. Her cousin, who lived in Bel Air, helped her get the job. It was a job that was more in line with the type of work she did in Frankfurt. The daily two-hour commute didn't seem to faze her at all. She viewed the situation as killing two birds with one stone; building up her driving experience, while working at a job she liked. I promised her that we would move to Los Angeles when I graduated from college.

Six months later, Gitta switched employment yet again. This time, she transferred to a more reputable company in the banking industry. Each move was a step in upward mobility. She had relocated to America and hit the ground running. Watching her in action progressing by leaps and bounds, I couldn't help but be inspired.

With everything I had on the line, my determination to achieve my goal was laser sharp. There was absolutely nothing that could stop me, not even my old mindset.

In his book *Unleash the Power Within*, Anthony Robbins writes, "A belief is an absolute certainty."

It's a powerful statement because I learned from experience that absolute certainty is very rare, if at all. And what if a particular belief just happens to be dead wrong, what then? One belief I always had was the idea that "A" students were naturally born smart. This view stemmed from the bad habits I had developed early on in my youth. As well-meaning as my grandmother had been in encouraging me to do well in school, she couldn't really do more to help me excel. I grew up in an environment that didn't foster education. Grandma never went to school, my three uncles never passed fourth grade, and Mom had only reached sixth grade. None of my family had the academic background to judge how I was really doing in school. They probably assumed I must have been getting a proper education, since I was physically in school.

In reality, I never bothered to do my homework or study for exams; I was satisfied if I got a C. Everyone in my circle of friends, with very few exceptions, treated school the same way. I assumed that everyone was just as ill-prepared as I was, and those who have gotten better grades were just naturally smarter than the rest of us. It took me until I was in my mid-twenties to slowly learn the correlation between preparation and favorable outcome.

For most people, this fact may seem too obvious to miss, but given my background of having no academic guidelines or discipline, this discovery was significant. As a full-time college student, juggling classes, projects, and exams, was a challenge. I had to learn new habits on how to organize, manage, and prioritize my time and resources in order to get optimum grades. It's a habit that continues to serve me well today.

Another valuable lesson learned during my tenure was the idea that in order to reach a well-informed conclusion, one must take the time to listen to both sides of the argument. Theoretically, I understood and agreed with its premise, but in practice, I never applied it. I learned the wisdom of this lesson the hard way during my Political Science presentation. The topic I had chosen for this project was the ongoing debate in the Philippines, at the time, about whether or not to renew the leases of the American military bases, Subic Naval Base and Clark Air Force Base.

I took the easy route by automatically making a judgment call in favor of extending the lease and keep the U.S. bases operating. I did exactly the opposite of what I was supposed to do - I made my conclusion first, and then gathered evidence to support my argument. I visualized myself stepping up at the podium, laying out my conclusion, providing ample evidence, and watch my classmates nod and agree, all the while in awe. Besides, I was the lone Filipino student in class. My classmates wouldn't know anything about the Philippines, and why would they even care?

When the moment arrived, I swaggered my way to the podium with confidence - judging David was easy prey for Goliath. I stated my conclusion that it was in the best interest of the Filipino people for the American military bases to remain in Philippine territory, and then I preceded to layout the following arguments:

First, removing the bases would render the Philippines vulnerable to foreign invasion. I cited the case in World War II when Japan invaded the Philippines, and highlighted, that for decades, the two bases have provided solid protection and deterrent to would-be foreign invaders.

Secondly, leasing these properties to the American government provided economic relief to the Philippine economy. Closing the bases down would mean a huge loss of revenue to the Philippine government, and a devastating blow to the economy.

And finally, thousands of jobs created by the military bases would be lost. Unemployment would rise, delivering another severe blow to the local economy. For these reasons, it's clear to see that the permanent closure of these military installations would be a colossal mistake.

Satisfied with my performance, I had a silly grin on my face when I opened the session for questioning. I was puzzled to see lots of hands quickly shot-up in the air. One by one, my classmates countered, point-by-point, and dismantled my arguments to pieces, exposing the weaknesses and fallacies of my reasoning.

One of them refuted that an argument could be made against my first point, that it was actually the strong American presence in the Philippines that prompted Japan to attack the region more heavily than anywhere else in the Pacific. Disputing that the grave destruction Japan inflicted on the Philippines wouldn't have been necessary if the Americans weren't there. Another classmate chimed-in to point out that the Philippines is a member the United Nations, and would be under its protection in the event of foreign invasion.

For my second point, another student brought to my attention that the so-called "rent" the Americans were paying to the Philippine government, came in the form of military hardware. He argued that what the Filipino people needed were decent jobs, not more guns. Furthermore, he asserted that even if these military weapons were sold for monetary gains, because of the country's rampant corruption, none of the money would ever funnel down to the public sector where it's needed most.

For my final point, someone remarked that the type of employment the military brought-in, consisted mostly of menial jobs; cooks, janitors, gardeners, and even worse, prostitutions. My classmate reasoned that Filipinos deserved better, and by placing them in charge of their own destiny, they could do a better job of attracting foreign investors who would hire skilled laborers.

When everything was said and done, it was apparent to everyone that I was completely unprepared. I couldn't even dispute the validity of their counterarguments, since I never bothered to do any research to consider the other side of the issue. I felt like a complete idiot in front of my entire class. And rather than trying to defend my self-imposed failure, I simply acknowledged the good points they've made, and quietly concluded my presentation.

Another significant observation I made during my college years was of the stark contrasts in the ways American and Filipino courses are conducted. My recollection of Filipino schools was of monologue system, where teachers lecture and students are expected to mechanically take notes, and the course requires plenty of memorization - learning by note.

American schools, I noticed, place more emphasis on critical thinking, problem solving, and innovation. The common requirements in most of the projects I worked on were: here's the challenge, identify the problem, come up with a solution, and sell the class on it. For a man of my background, conditioned only to receive and follow instructions, these tasks were monumentally challenging. Engaging in this form of exercises forced me to think outside of my comfort zone and probe new ideas and create realistic solutions to problems. Developing the skill set to stand before a crowd and sell them on the merits of my work was another tool that had practical usefulness in the real world.

There were also lessons to be learned outside the classroom. As a business major, I thought it was crucial for me to gain some sales experience while still in school. I wanted to see if the theoretical lessons I've learned can be applied to practical business situations. To achieve this goal I decided to take the summer off from school and try my hand at corporate sales. I wanted to really challenge myself, and deliberately went after a sales position in an ultra-competitive environment. I found the ideal job working full time at a car dealership, a pure commission-based position.

Through that experience, I discovered that I had a knack for prospecting potential clients and enjoyed the challenge of finding the automobile that best suited their needs and budgets. What I didn't like about the experience was the sleazy way in which this car dealership conducted business. I am not suggesting in any way that all car dealerships operate in the same manner. But at this particular dealership, the salespeople were encouraged to make false promises to customers in order to lure them into the Sales Manager's office, whose main role was to hammer the customer into submission.

This dealership employed many twisted tactics. One such strategy was to literally hold the clients captive at the negotiation table for a prolonged period of time, sometimes eight hours or longer. The idea was to wear down the customers to the point where they would agree to sign any contract just to get out of there. The business model of this particular dealership, which bordered on deception and coercion, was completely bizarre. They hadn't taught me these practices in school.

We would have motivational Friday morning meetings to pump up the sales force for the weekend sales drive. This meeting was conducted by the General Manager Sean Thomas, a slender, bookish man in his late thirties. On the surface, he appeared timid, but when he got on the sales floor, he would turn into an entertaining snake oil sales man. I could not believe the crazy things that would come out of Sean's mouth. He'd say things like, "Outside that door are customers with your money in their pockets. Yes, that's right! That money belongs to you, and your job is to dig deep in their pockets and take your money back."

By the end of these meetings, the sales force would be so whirled up that we felt like we could sell ice cubes to Eskimos.

There was no system in place of peacefully pairing customers with salespeople. Instead, dozens of us would stand around on the sidewalk like vultures, eagerly waiting for someone to pull over. The rule was whoever claims it first, gets it. I saw salespeople literally tripping over each other to get to a customer. I found myself chasing cars before they had even pulled over, yelling, "I got this, I got this!"

Prompting other salesman to come out of the woodwork claiming, "No, I got this first. I saw them from a block away."

The intimidating, mob-like atmosphere of the dealership could easily make any customer feel apprehensive. It was not uncommon for them to start by saying, "I don't want any pressure. I'm just looking."

I quickly learned to deflect this kind of objection by saying, "Mr. Customer, the only pressure you'll get from me is what you see inside those tires."

Then I'd follow them around like a puppy; otherwise, other salesman would take over immediately.

Part of the negotiation phase was to con the customers into thinking the salesman was on their side. This trick was used to set them up with the goal of eventually convincing them that their demands were unreasonable. I remember a negotiation that lasted for nearly eight hours, and reach a point when the customer finally relented and said, "Screw it! Where do I sign? I just want to get out of here."

Despite the zoo like atmosphere, I did sell 30 vehicles in my first month at the dealership. In the two months of working there that summer, I befriended several of my colleagues. They were a fun bunch to be around, but the unethical way the company conducted its business turned me off completely.

The following year, I saw an article in the local paper about the GM's arrest. Sean had been charged with embezzlement, resulting in the dealership permanently closing its doors. The irony of how he was ultimately captured was hilarious.

During my first week working for Sean the year prior, he summoned me to his office and introduced me to his best friend from high school. Sean winked at me and said, "Ben, take good care of my best buddy."

I took his wink to mean to treat this man like any other customer. We engaged in lengthy conversations while we waited for several hours for the finance office to complete his deal. At some point, the discussion turned to his relationship with Sean; how long they'd been friends, and spoke highly of Sean's outstanding work ethic. He relayed that in their teens, whenever Sean mowed his parents' lawn, he'd end-up mowing all the lawns on the entire block, for free. He recalled, "Everyone in the neighborhood loved Sean's boundless energy and generosity."

When Sean became a fugitive of the law, everyone who knew him, myself included, presumed he must have been somewhere in the Bahamas already, basking in the sun and sipping fancy cocktails with colorful little umbrellas. But when the authorities finally caught up with him, we were all surprised to learn that he never left town. All along, Sean had been hiding at a relative's home.

While in hiding, Sean decided to mow the lawn one day, probably out of boredom. When he was done, he went on to mow the lawn of the next door neighbor, and then the next, and the next. He was well on his way to mowing every lawn in the block, when one of the neighbors heard the mower in his yard and took a look. He recognized Sean from a picture in the newspaper, and called the police. When I read the story of how he was captured, I immediately remembered the day I sold a car to his best friend.

The following summer, I found another job at a bank. I started as a teller and quickly made my way to a position selling home equity loans. Banks are highly regulated, and conducted themselves with high ethical standards for their dealings with the public. I liked working in complete transparency with clients, no high-pressure sales, and the pride of knowing customers hadn't been tricked into anything. I liked the job so much that I continued working part time when school resumed in the fall. By the time I graduated the following summer, I had already made up my mind that a career in sales was what I wanted to pursue.

In June 1993, I graduated with a Bachelor degree in Business Administration. It was a milestone achievement for me. I had accomplished something that no one on my mother's side of the family had ever accomplished. I only wished Grandma Rufina was present that day, she would have been really proud of me. But still, Gitta, along with my daughters, and the rest of my family were there to celebrate the momentous day.

As promised, a couple of weeks after my graduation ceremony, Gitta and I packed our belongings and moved to Los Angeles. We found a rustic two bedroom apartment in Glendale, and after a week of settling in, I hit the ground running in search of employment.

Being fresh out of college, I approached the employment search enthusiastically. However, my idealistic zeal was quickly dampened by the deep recession in the summer of 1993; there weren't many companies hiring. It took several months of knocking on doors and attending job fairs before a bank finally hired me in a Junior Sales position selling home equity loans and other bank products and services. The salary was not what I expected, but I was just glad to be employed and on the road to building a career. My goal was to eventually get into real estate finance.

Glendale was an ideal location for both Gitta and me. Her office was located in downtown Los Angeles, and mine in Pasadena. My early years working in corporate America brought me to the realization that my line of thinking was not where it needed to be. Beneath the surface, I was still operating under the mindset of my old conditioning. I didn't want to make waves or offend anyone, so I obeyed authority passively and did as I was told.

My behavior was brought to my attention by my Branch Manager, Tim Myers. He was a soft spoken man in his early forties whose features reminded me of the legendary film maker Woody Allen. He summoned me to his office one day after our morning meeting and voiced his concern over my apparent lack of interest in participating in group discussions. He started the conversation with, "I've noticed that when I ask for your input in our meetings, you don't have much to say, and on the rare occasions when you did, you always sugar coat things as if everything is going well."

Apparently, my boss viewed me as the least contributing member in our team when it came to sharing new ideas and information about market conditions. Undoubtedly, he derived his conclusion from the passive way I had conducted myself during these meetings. His assessment of my conduct couldn't have been further from the truth. In reality, I had plenty to say, but I dreaded open forum meetings which, to me, could lead to open confrontation. I hadn't realized that in actuality, I was still carrying on with my old Filipino mindset which viewed public display of disagreement as something that must be avoided. I didn't feel comfortable openly voicing my opinions for fear of offending my colleagues or superiors. For me, it was a cultural issue, but my boss saw it as lack of interest. Worse yet, he probably thought I was incompetent.

I didn't want to admit to my boss that the difficulty I faced was cultural; I feared that he may not understand, or that he might think that cultural conflict couldn't be overcome. My immediate reaction was to instinctively tap into my Filipino mindset of wanting to respect and please my superior. Once again, I sugar-coated my thoughts and just said, "You're absolutely right. I will be more assertive in our next meeting."

Tim calmly said, "Ben, don't be so quick to just passively agree with me. What I want to hear from you is some real input, what's really on your mind. You're not helping by just agreeing with me. You're my eyes and ears for what goes on in the market place. You know our customers - their concerns, the areas we need to improve in, how we compare against our competitors, and so on. I need you to be assertive and tell me what I need to know - not what I want to hear."

It was this conversation that really prompted me to reexamine my value system of what I believed to be the right thing to do: being humble, not make waves, and avoid offending anyone. I began to understand that my old conditioning was in direct conflict with what my new environment required of me. My boss was clearly telling me that I needed to change and get on with the program.

To me, cultural change means abandoning my deeply held belief system; one that I know so well and comfortable in. Internally, cultural change is a monumental task because it requires the rewiring of what I already knew, and replace it with a different mindset that's strangely outside of my comfort zone. However, if I wanted to succeed in an American corporate environment, I didn't really have much of a choice but to assimilate in it.

At Tim's behest, I made a sincere effort to participate in our weekly meetings; I forced myself to be as candid and truthful in sharing my observations and suggestions. Initially, the task of being "frank" was excruciatingly uncomfortable. I even stuttered at times. I had made a lifetime habit of sugar coating everything I said that it became an incredibly difficult habit to break.

The more encouragement I received from my boss and peers, the better I felt about my new behavior. Eventually, I reached a point where expressing my point of view in a tactful manner became second nature; I no longer needed to sugar coat what I had to say. Naturally, I remained respectful toward my seniors, but I no longer held figures of authority in great awe, the way I did before.

Overcoming this particular cultural obstacle made me realize that many of the difficulties I encountered in the past had been the products of deep cultural differences. It was an ongoing discovery I would find as I continued to make my way into the American corporate world.

On the home front, life with Gitta was wonderful. We each pursued our own career path which kept us very busy during the work week. However, at the end of each day, we established a routine to unwind over dinner and a glass of wine. We mutually agreed that I would do the cooking, and she would be responsible for doing the dishes. It was arrangement that ran like clockwork. When we get home from work, she'd pour us each a glass of wine, while I prepared the evening meal, and we'd immerse ourselves in discussions about the day's event.

I brought up the topic of corporate loyalty during one of our nightly table discussions. I had learned a lot about the Western mentality by observing the way my wife dealt and coped with the challenges she faced at work. Previously, the only real job I'd ever had was my tenure in the U.S. Army. I had always viewed company loyalty as something sacred. It's a system where everyone wins: my employer would have the security of knowing that no matter what happened, I could be counted on to stay with the company, and likewise, I could rest assured that my employer would always be there for me. In my mind, this arrangement made perfect sense.

My outlook on company loyalty was perfectly aligned with my collective point of view. Even though I was convinced that leaving the military was the right decision for me, admittedly, I did feel guilty when I resigned. I simply embraced the notion of "quid pro quo."

What prompted me to bring this discussion to the dinner table was the contrast of mine and Gitta's outlook on the topic. I noticed that she simply did not share my attitude when dealing with her employers. Gitta completely disagreed with my take on corporate loyalty, and had no qualms about transferring from one company to another. She held the view that devotion to one company may not necessarily serve one's own best interest. In the past, such a mindset may have been the norm, but the modern corporate world no longer functioned in the same manner; it now worked like a cold machine.

In her observations, companies operated from a bottom line perspective, and treated workers like tools. If a new position was needed, for example, the company would simply fill it. When the position did not live up to expectation in its contribution to the company's bottom line, it was simply eliminated without any second thoughts.

Gitta reasoned that with globalization well under way, contemporary workers had to come to terms with the fact that in today's working environment, everyone is expendable. And rather than being at the mercy of the company, Gitta argued, workers have to think like a company does and look out for their own best interests. And that, individually, each of us has to continually improve on our skill sets and expertise to put ourselves in a position to pick and choose which company we want to work for.

Logically, Gitta's line of reasoning made sense, but once again, my old internal wiring vehemently resisted the idea. The next evening, as a followed-up to our previous discussion, she gave me a book - a paperback by Jerrold Mundis called **Earn What You Deserve.**

Our nightly ritual at the dining table served as our private refuge to unwind and let go the stresses of the day. We'd often get carried away with our conversation and stay up talking past midnight. We would wake up the next day feeling refreshed, revitalized, and ready to take on the world. There was a comfort in knowing that no matter what the day brings, we always had the sanctuary of our nightly ritual to come home to.

Then one night, eight years into our relationship, Gitta brought up an unexpected topic at the dinner table - her desire to have a child. The subject completely caught me by surprise. We've had this discussion at length before and clearly clarified my stance on this issue. Gitta knew and accepted my not wanting to have any more children; but now, in her mid-thirties, she has had a change of heart.

Initially, I was at a loss for words and didn't know what to say. On the one hand, I knew without a doubt that Gitta would make an excellent mother. On the other hand, I was still adamant about not wanting any more children. Obviously, this decision had so much riding on it. I asked Gitta to give me some time to seriously think it over, before rendering my decision. She agreed, and we set a date to resume the discussion. What started out as just another ordinary evening, turned out to be a major turning point in our relationship.

In the days that followed, a cultural battle raged inside me. The echoes of my Filipino heritage rang loudly in my head; the need of self-sacrifice for the greater good. While the American side of me insisted on staying true to myself, and stand by my conviction. There was no question that she'd be exceptional as a mother, and I certainly did not want to deny the privilege of having Gitta as the future child's mother.

Whichever I decide, there were downsides to consider either way. I did not want to have lifelong arguments with Gitta over having a child against my will, nor did I want her to live in resentment for denying her the privilege of motherhood. Ultimately, no matter how much I tried to refute or rationalize how I felt, deep down inside, the truth remains that I simply did not want to have any more children. It was a fact I could not deny even if I tried.

A week later as planned, Gitta and I drove to our favorite hiking trail at the Griffith Park observatory to continue our discussion. As we hiked up the hill, I spoke in great length of the thought process I had gone through in reaching my decision. I wanted her to know that I'd given her request the utmost of consideration. Likewise, she reiterated all of the reasons she had cited during our original discussion. Our passionate exchange went on for the duration of our hike, and concluded just as we reached the trail's summit.

At the edge of the lookout post, we paused for a moment, trying to catch our breath. I marveled momentarily at the magnificent panoramic view of the Los Angeles basin below. Breaching the brief silence, Gitta asked, "Have you made a decision?"

I took a moment to take a deep breath, knowing that what I was about to say would change the trajectory of our lives. "Yes, I have. I would have loved to spend the rest of my life with you, but I can't give you what you yearn for. But I love you enough to let you go, if having a child is what you really want."

I was hoping Gitta would say that she'd think it over further, but apparently, she had already made up her mind. "I, too, have made my decision. I want a child. And though I accept and respect your decision, it makes me very sad that you will not be a part of our lives."

As we made the two-mile trek back to the parking lot, the tone of finality gradually worked its way to the realization that soon, Gitta and I would no longer be together. Neither of us uttered a single word on our way down. A decision had been reached; there was nothing left to say.

All my life, I had lived according to the cultural norms of what was expected of me. As a husband, I should have adhered to my wife's needs. From a Filipino perspective, I had committed a selfish act by walking away from the commitment to my wife. The American side in me, however, begged to differ. Bringing a life into this world is a colossal responsibility and one that should never be taken half-heartedly. And that's how I would feel if I forced myself to commit to something I honestly did not want to do. My old cultural codes were fading, and I have changed.

In the fall of 1996, Gitta and I were divorced and she relocated back to Germany. She explained that the only reason why she moved to Los Angeles was to be with me, and now that we're apart, she no longer had a reason to stay. Gitta regained her former employment in Frankfurt and was later reassigned to the bank's London office. And it was there, she met an English man she would eventually marry, and with whom she would have a child.

CHAPTER 11

THE CONSUMMATE UNDERDOG

"The greatest danger for most of us is not that we aim too high and miss it – but we aim too low and reach it."

- Michael Angelo

***

In my late thirties, I thought I had fully adapted to the American culture. However, I was unaware that certain traits from my collectivist upbringing were still lodged deep within my psyche. One trait in particular, was my negative view of self-promotion. The presence of this characteristic was so subtle and faint that I hadn't noticed it had been there all along. Similar to an unresolved issue, it lingered just beneath the surface of my skin, patiently waiting there for the right trigger to awaken it and exert its powerful influence on my behavior.

My initial cultural conditioning naturally lends itself to embrace the virtues of self-restraint and reverence to humility. I was raised in a society that discouraged making waves and frowned self-promotion. Americans, on the other hand, have no qualms about making waves. They're loud, boisterous, and have no reservation when it comes to expressing what's on their minds. They have the same prevailing attitude when it comes to self-promotion; they will not hesitate when it comes to advancing their own self-interest.

When pursuing promotions, for example, Americans are expected to openly talk-up to superiors about their expectations, goals, capabilities, and achievements. For someone like me, conditioned to view self-promotion as greedy and self-serving, following the American procedure to get promoted was difficult. Unaware of these cultural changes in attitude, I blindly continued my humble approach; I did my job quietly and effectively, believing that it was my manager's responsibility to notice and recommend me for the next promotion.

The virtue of humility certainly has its merits in an American social setting, but I soon discovered that applying it also to an American business setting can have an adverse result. It's a consequence I took notice of during my tenure at Richardson Steel, the largest steel distributor in the United States. The company was formed in 1849 and had weathered the ups and downs of economic turmoil in the United States for over 150 years. I was proud to be a part of this great company, rich in history and achievements. I started my career there in 1997.

Richardson Steel sponsored a program at the prestigious University of Southern California, which provided the company with ample candidates for hire. I was hired despite my status as a non-USC graduate, and in spite of my apparent lack of technical knowledge of the steel industry. The General Manager who conducted my job interview was a man by the name of Frank Antoine. He liked how I conducted myself and believed I would be a good addition to their sales team. Frank assured me that I would have no problem learning the technical aspect of the job in due time, but that having good people skill was an ability that could not be taught, a quality that he apparently saw in me.

I began my employment with Richardson Steel along with two other recruits; Sally and Charlie, both recent USC graduates in their mid-twenties. The three of us began as Inside Sales representatives, taking incoming calls and servicing customers. I was assigned to handle the small accounts: mom-and-pop-type establishments, shoppers, and low-potential customers with purchasing power of $10,000-$50,000 per year. These types of accounts required some sales efforts to get them to buy. I viewed this assignment as a perfect training ground to sharpen my sales skills.

On the contrary, Sally and Charlie were assigned to handle the contractual accounts; major customers with purchasing power of over a million dollars. These were customers under contract to buy only from us. These accounts required less sales effort on behalf of the Inside Sales representative and had more with keeping track of inventory levels and order entries. Out of a dozen Inside Sales reps in the department, I was the only one who was assigned to handle non-contractual accounts.

The arrangements didn't bother me at first, until I learned how the company tracked and presented individual's performance. Inside Sales reps were pitted against each other by way of who can produce the highest sales revenue. This system placed me at a great disadvantage since I was limited to only handling small accounts, as opposed to the established big accounts the rest of my colleagues handled. I was doomed to always be behind my colleagues in the performance report that management distributed in the sales office at the end of each month.

I'm naturally competitive, so I hated being last on the sales performance list. The lopsided set up became even more apparent when I attended our first annual corporate meeting. Our boss, Frank Antoine, announced how pleased he was with the new recruit's sales performances for the year, and he specifically mentioned Sally and Charlie. There was no mention of me. I was humiliated and felt like an outcast.

As the months went by, the gap between my sales figure and the figures of my colleagues became even wider. While I continued working on developing my small accounts, Sally and Charlie were building solid relationships with their contractual accounts. These were important accounts, and the Outside Sales representatives often invited Sally and Charlie to accompany them on sales calls, to meetings with key customers, plant tours, cocktails, dining, and attending Lakers games. Our company had season tickets to the Lakers; they were excellent seats in the third row and dead center. But such special treats were only extended to our million-dollar customers, which I didn't have.

I couldn't help but feel resentment over Sally and Charlie being groomed to succeed while I was being ignored. I was especially resentful towards Charlie, who seemed to shamelessly brag about large orders he booked or complements he received from his customers. Worst of all, Frank seemed to embrace this kind of behavior with pride.

Unexpectedly one day, the Inside Sales Department initiated a new incentive program. Anyone who made a sale over $2,000 with a profit margin of 25% would receive $5 per order as reward. It seemed miniscule, but I saw it as a huge opportunity to shine. I was happy to hear that the highest performing participant would be announced on a weekly basis. Individual effort, regardless of account type, would now be recognized and rewarded, leveling-out the playing field.

The incentive program lasted for a couple of months, and I consistently came out on top with the highest profit margin and total volume of sales. The consistency of my name at the top of the weekly list eventually caught the attention of the Western Division President, Ron Lombard. Even our general manager, Frank Antoine, would sometimes drop by my cubicle to comment on the remarkable job I was doing. At one point, he went as far to tell me, "I had a long talk with Ron Lombard about your excellent performance, and it looks like the sun is going to finally shine your way. But don't mention it to anyone just yet."

I was ecstatic, especially hearing it directly from Frank. In my mind, Frank was doing what a boss should do, notice the hard work of his subordinate and talk me up to his boss. Things were finally working out as I had envisioned.

CULTURE CLASH

Two years into my career with the company, I felt that I was ready to take on a new responsibility - I wanted an Outside Sales position. The face-to-face interaction with clients and the challenge of developing a territory from nothing into multimillion-dollar accounts excited me. I wanted a shot at making a six figure salary, having a company car, and the perks that come with the great responsibility. It's a career goal that I shared with the General Manager on several occasions.

Shortly after the incentive program ended, Frank called me in to his office and offered me a new assignment. The Inside Sales Department in our San Francisco branch was in the process of consolidating their operations to our Los Angeles facility. The San Francisco warehouse would continue its function and keep its outside sales force in the Bay Area, but all incoming sales calls would be diverted to Los Angeles. The San Francisco inside sales team was offered the option to relocate to Los Angeles, but none of them were willing to transfer.

I was offered a position as part of the new team to handle the San Francisco division. The news was not what I had hoped for; I'd still be doing inside sales, just covering a different region. However, Frank, in his usual convincing way, insisted that this important project would be closely monitored by corporate headquarters. And with all eyes cast on this project, it provides an excellent opportunity for me to shine. He emphasized this was a stepping stone that will bring me closer to my goal. Frank was absolutely confident that if the project proved to be a success, I would surely be rewarded. With my bosses' assurances, I gladly accepted the challenge.

The San Francisco program progressed with ease. The transition had only minimal disruption and was hardly noticeable to our existing customers. We didn't even lose any clients in the process. In fact, once the transition settled down, we began to gain more customers and expanded the range of our territory.

Approximately three months into the program, I learned through conversation with Frank's secretary that he had just promoted Charlie to an outside sales position. I was livid; I wasn't even made aware that a position had opened. In the back of my mind, I've always had the nagging suspicion that Frank never really cared about looking-out for my best interest. I wanted to give him the benefit of the doubt and restrained myself from entertaining such a thought, but with this latest development, all my doubts had been removed. Frank had made me believe that I was next in line for the promotion, and I had been passed over underhandedly.

Even in highly emotional charged state, I was still reluctant to confront Frank. My hesitation had more to do with cultural reverence towards respect for authority figures. I stewed over the incident for several days, and it was eating me alive inside. I reached a point where it started to affect my attitude. Even my customers detected the change in me, and that was not acceptable. I had to come up with a constructive way to channel my frustrations over what I considered a deliberate deceit on Frank's part. Something had to be done about it, and that something required me to go outside of my comfort zone. I would have to confront my superior.

I appeared at my boss's door and requested a moment of his time. Frank was very accommodating and offered me a seat as I entered his office. Unbeknownst to me at the time, my inside sales supervisor had already forewarned Frank about the issue I wanted to discuss. Frank wasted no time and directly addressed the issue at hand. "I understand that you have some concerns about your future with Richardson Steel. I want you to know that you can always come directly to me with any problems or issues that you want to talk about. Furthermore, I want to point out that your contribution to our team is highly valued. You are a valuable asset to the company, Ben. However, your availability for the new opening in outside sales was somewhat limited, primarily due to the significance of your involvement with the San Francisco project. So I made the decision to give the position to Charlie instead, but I can assure you that it had nothing to do with me thinking you weren't qualified for the position. I know that you are. I promise you that your turn will come."

As always, Frank sounded sincere and convincing, but I had heard those assurances many times before. I replied, "I find it ironic that the reason why I agreed to take the San Francisco project was because you had assured me it would bring me closer to my goal. Now you're telling me that the reason I didn't get the job this time is because I did what you advised me to do."

I continued, "By now, I am thoroughly convinced that management does not have any interest in my career goal within this company. And when I say management, I am referring to you, Frank. Having said it, I want you to also know that I've decided to pursue my Master's program while working full time in my current position."

Frank retorted, "Well, that changes the whole scenario. In that case, I can't give you the promotion if you're in school. You'll wind up doing your school work instead of doing your job."

I defiantly said, "Frank, once I commit to my Master's program I'll be too busy focusing on school, I won't need your promotion. I've made up my mind, and that's what I intend to do. You can take me off of your list for the next couple of years."

Frank calmly said, "Maybe we need to discuss this further, with more time than we have at this moment."

At that point, Frank rushed out of the office and went to his next meeting. I went back to my desk with the satisfaction of having a load of frustrations off of my chest.

Later that day, I received a voice mail message from Ron Lombard, "Hey, Ben, I heard about your dilemma. I just want you to know that I think the world of you, and for the President of the company to think that highly of you - can't be all that bad. For as long as I am in charge, your career with the company will always be safe. Call me if you want to talk."

The message from Ron meant a lot to me. His support reinforced my sense of loyalty to the company and the bond I had developed with the people I worked with. This type of gesture is what kept me hanging on with the company, especially in times when I felt my career was not going anywhere.

For the next two years, I immersed myself in my Master's program at the University of Redland's Burbank campus. Richardson Steel's tuition reimbursement program was generous, but the company also wanted to make sure that I was serious about my studies. The company was willing to pay 90% of tuition if I got an A, 50% for a B, and an automatic disqualification from the program if I ever got a C. In return, if and when I graduated from the Master's program, I was obligated to stay with the company for two years as return on their investment in my education.

The two-year program was non-stop; once I started, there were no breaks. I had papers due every week, and I only had the weekends to work on them. Needless to say, for a couple of years, I had no social life. I plowed into the program while holding my full time job. I breezed right though the first year, but by the time I reached the last six months, I was getting burned out. However, I still managed to complete the program and in June of 2003, I received my Master's Degree in Business Management.

In a nutshell, what I learned from the master's program was the importance of seeing the big picture, the bird's eye view. As leaders, seeing the totality of what's ahead is crucial in moving a company forward through the rough economic terrains of the unforeseeable future. The participants of my program were a mix of managers from different industries; pharmaceutical, oil and energy, aerospace, automotive, media, entrepreneurs, and even professionals from the government sector.

Ideas and theories from textbooks were often met with scrutiny from my classmates. The classroom was an open forum where merits were either taken apart or vouched for. Someone might say, "Yeah, in our department, we've tried something very similar and it turned out to be a total failure. Here's why…"

Or someone would say the opposite.

In one of our open discussions, someone brought up the topic of fairness in the workplace. My classmate, a sales manager from a pharmaceutical company, gave the example of someone in her department who had filed a formal complaint against her for not giving him a promotion.

Candidate A, she said, had worked as an inside sales rep for some time. He did as well as could be expected for someone in that position, but the promotion he was after required a different set of skills. Candidate B did a much better job of demonstrating that he had the right qualifications for an outside sales position. She felt that Candidate A was not aggressive enough, which is a crucial part of being on the road. She explained, "It's not my job to hand him the promotion. He has to convince me that he's got what it takes. If he wanted the job badly enough, he should have showed me!"

Her statement grabbed my attention because it came so close to home. She had described my dilemma at work - I hadn't been able to convince my boss to give me the promotion I wanted. My classmate's example caused me to ask myself if I had really shown my boss that I had what it took to get the job done.

In all honesty, I couldn't say that I did. I had relied on the assumption that it was my boss's responsibility to take notice of my good work performance. If I had to bring it up to his attention, I wouldn't feel comfortable with it; I'd feel like I was bragging. Tooting my own horn is something I never felt comfortable doing; in fact, I loathed people who acted self-servingly.

I began to dig deeper to understand why I felt so negatively about advancing one's self-interest. Time and time again, it all came down to my cultural belief in humility. When I questioned myself further as to why that was? My answer was always, "That's how it was in the Philippines."

Obviously, such mentality is perfectly legit if I was still in the Philippines, but I'm not. I'm doing myself a great disservice by continuing with the limitations of the old ways, a mentality that is not conducive in a highly competitive American business setting. It goes back again to Anthony Robbins' previous statement about "absolute certainty." I had never bothered to question my deep reverence for humility, for in my mind, it had always been an absolute certainty.

I was also reminded of the discussion I once had with Gitta over dinner, when she tried to make me see that my dislike for promoting one's own self-interest in the workplace was, in fact, misguided. Her point of view never resonated with me because I was absolute certain that I was right.

The woman in my class never knew the profound impact her statement had made. I tried to remember my previous efforts to promote my own agenda, and realized I never really made any. I entrusted others with the task of looking out for my best interest, a responsibility that in American culture was squarely my own. This disconnect, which I hadn't noticed before, had cost me many opportunities for promotion. For the first time in my professional career, I understood the source of my shortcomings.

I had been particularly hard on my colleague Charlie and looked down on him as the ultimate self-promoter, shameless, and conspicuously greedy. When in fact, Charlie only did what

CULTURE CLASH

one does in an "individualist" culture; it was not only acceptable, but expected. I could have raised my concerns at the very beginning when I thought I was getting the crappy accounts and Charlie was getting the good ones. But I chose not to, and allowed my distorted belief to hold me back

Logically, I understood the change I need to do, but emotionally, every fiber in my body resisted the idea with fierce ferocity. Truth was staring me in the eye, if I want to be an outside sales rep, I'll have to convince my boss that I was the best qualified man for the job. I finally understood that there was no way around it. I'll have to find a way to come to terms with the inevitable change.

Strategically, I thought it would be far more convincing if a third party was to notify my boss about my good performance. Whenever a customer complimented me for a job well done, I would nervously ask, "Why don't you mention that to my boss next time you talk to him?"

I would say it jokingly at first, because it helped ease the discomfort I felt in saying it. I did this for some time until I reached a point where I didn't feel the need to disguise my intentions anymore. I heard somewhere that if something is repeated 21 times, it becomes a habit. I don't know the validity of the specific number 21, but I do know that repetition forms habit, and an ingrained habit provides ease.

The flow of compliments on my behalf steadily funneled through to Frank's attention. I encouraged not only my customers to spread the word to my boss, but also the outside sales reps, especially Charlie, who surprised me by complying gladly. I started to get random calls from Frank to acknowledge the excellent work I was doing.

Then one day, I was tipped off by our company president that Frank was in the process of interviewing candidates for an outside sales position in the Inland Empire, 50 miles east of Los

Angeles. I informed Frank of my interest in being a candidate for the new position. Frank agreed to interview me the following morning.

I have had several interviews with Frank in the past, and they all had the same predictable outcome of getting passed over. I walked into his office, fully expecting his demeanor to be the same as it had been every other time. What Frank didn't know was that this time, I was operating under a different mindset and was fully prepared for the inevitable rejection.

Just as I had anticipated, Frank started to let me down before I could even utter a single word. He said, "Ben, I'm not going to give you the position this time. Before I tell you why, I would like to mention the positive things about your performance..."

He went on to explain, "There are two reasons why I've decided not to promote you this time around. One, the territory is out of your way. The Inland Empire is too far from your home in Glendale. Two, this is serious. I have observed that you always come to work late, and I just can't have that."

I sat there quietly while he went on and on with his long-winded speech. When he finally finished, I asked, "Frank, would you at least allow me to express why I strongly feel I deserve this promotion?"

Frank reluctantly agreed as he crossed his arms and, literally, rolled his eyes at me. "Yeah, sure, go ahead."

His gesture suggested that I needed to make it quick, so I plunged right into my rebuttal. "First of all, your concern about me being out of geographical range is a non-issue. I am willing to relocate to the Inland Empire at my own expense. Secondly, I know the territory very well because I am from there; I attended Fontana High School, got my bachelor's degree at Cal State San Bernardino, and my Master's degree at University of Redlands.

Chances are, most of the decision-makers in that area are probably people I'm already acquainted with. Another thing, Frank, I am very familiar with this territory because I handled it for three years on the inside sales desk."

I went on to mention a few major accounts in the area that I used to handle.

His eyes lit up. "Yeah!"

I continued, "As far as my qualifications, I feel I am highly qualified for the job. For five years, I sat at that inside sales desk and learned from the best. I know the computer system very well, and if I don't know the answer to any problems, I know the resources within the company where I can find the solution. I get along with everyone and always maintain a positive attitude because I'm a firm believer that when it comes to progress, attitude is everything. But best of all, my strength is in my ability to communicate. You've seen me in action in the impromptu speeches I used to give at our weekly meetings."

He nodded in agreement. "You're absolutely right, Ben."

I smiled. "Frank, as long as I know the subject well, you can put me in front of a customer or a crowd and I can really do some damage."

He laughed.

I went on to say, "In regards to your second concern about my tardiness, I assure you that it will never happen again."

Frank interrupted me, saying, "I don't have time to babysit you, Ben."

I said, "Do you remember my first company interview with you, five years ago? Back then, you expressed your concern that you weren't sure of my intention to stay with the company in the long run. Do you recall that conversation?"

He said, "Yes, I do."

I persisted, "Back then, I assured you that I wanted a career and I was in it for the long haul. Five years later, I'm still here, Frank, just like I promised I would be. I feel that I have proven myself to be a man of my word. Now, as a man of my word, I promise you that my tardiness is the last thing you should ever have to worry about."

He paused for a moment before saying, "Ben, you give me a very convincing argument, but I'm still not sure."

At that point, I just simply asked him straight out, "Frank, does my word mean anything to you at all?"

Startled, he said, "Ben, I don't want you to feel dejected. I never knew how aggressive you could be in going after the position, and that's good."

I told him, "Frank, all my life, I've always been the consummate underdog. Everything I have accomplished, I've earned. I've had to fight for everything I have."

By then Frank's tone had softened considerably. "Ben, being an underdog is something that I can relate to because I, too, have walked a mile or two in your shoes. I'll be honest with you, Ben. When you walked through that door, I had already made up my mind on who to give the job to. But after having this discussion with you, I'm really having second thoughts. That speaks volumes of your persuasiveness."

My heart started pounding with excitement. I couldn't believe what I was hearing from Frank. He continued, "Here's what I'm going to do. I'm going to seriously reconsider my original decision. Give me until 4 p.m. today, and I will let you know my final decision."

I happily replied, "Fair enough, Frank."

Later that afternoon, Frank summoned me back to his office. "Ben, after careful consideration, I've decided to go with my original decision. However, in three months, you will be an outside sales representative. Your new territory will be in Los Angeles, so you won't have to relocate. As a man of my word, this I can promise you. How does it sound?"

I was so elated that I could have slam dunked a basketball. In the three months that followed, just as I had promised, I never came in late.

Ironically, Ron Lombard, the company President, threw a curve ball at me. He took me to lunch one day and offered me a different job; another special project that would take me away from the outside sales position I had my eye on. I told Ron that I had too much respect for him not to consider his offer, but that my heart was really set on the outside sales position. He agreed to give me some time to think it over.

I wanted the outside sales position more than anything, but I risk offending the President if I refused his offer. I went to Frank's office to seek his advice. He completely understood the tight spot I was in and was sympathetic of my predicament. He told me not to worry and assured me that his original offer was intact. Frank did me a huge favor by convincing Ron to find another candidate to fill the other position. Just as he had promised, the position that had eluded me for so long was finally mine. Frank kept his word.

It took me a long time to reach this milestone, but once I understood the culture, I set out to play by the rules and hit the right tone with the right people. I was able to win over my boss, who for five years, had virtually ignored and denied me every opportunity for promotion. In the end, not only that he kept his promise, Frank also persuaded the president to let me have the position I really wanted. I couldn't help but think that I could have gotten the job much earlier if I had adapted to my cultural environment sooner.

In the two years prior to his retirement in 2006, Frank became my mentor and showed me the ropes in the exciting world of sales. I couldn't have asked for better counsel than what I had under Frank's tutelage.

CHAPTER 12

EVOLVE: THE MAN I'VE BECOME

"It is never too late to be what you might have been."

- George Eliot

***

In the lottery of birth, we don't get to choose our parents, our economic status, or our race. We do the best we can with the circumstances we are born into. By random chance, I just happened to be born into an impoverished family in a Third-World country, along with the misfortune of having a father who chose not to be a part of my life. But even still, I consider myself fortunate for having had people in my life that deeply cared for me. The two in particular: my mother who did the best she could to pave the way for me to have a better chance in life, and Grandma Rufina who filled the glaring void by the absence of my parents during my formative years. The selfless sacrifices these two amazing women have made enabled me to enjoy the life I have today. No words can express the gratitude I feel.

Although I spent a good portion of my early years in abject poverty, the dignified people in the town I grew up in have more than compensated for what the town lacked economically. It was a place where everyone knew each other, and happiness was obtained by simply having food on the table, good health, and enclosed with loved ones. Alumnos was where I experienced the genuine warmth of friendship; a quality of closeness and sense of belonging that I have never experienced since, and perhaps - never will again.

The two main challenges that I struggled with in my early years in America, were the language and cultural barriers. At least with the language barrier, the problem was straightforward; I needed to learn to speak the English language. I knew where to get help; I could go to school or hire a tutor. However, the cultural barrier was far more complicated to decipher. For one thing, it's invisible. How could I have sought a solution to a problem I didn't even know existed?

Human nature as is, we tend to believe that the world we know so well inside our head is, or should be, universal. I was no exception; I also felt the same way. After all, the Filipino way was a world I knew inside and out, a culture I felt comfortable in, and experienced its effectiveness first hand. It seems only obvious that if it worked so well where I'm from, then the world I knew should be embraced anywhere else in the globe.

As an adult, I got too caught up with the struggle to earn a livelihood that, unknowingly, I continued to under estimate the adverse impact cultural differences can bring. But as we all know, sooner or later, reality will not be denied and exert itself intrusively in our lives. Slowly but surely, I eventually got the point. In time, through trial and error, I gained my foothold and assimilated into the American culture. I integrated so well, in fact, that I have become what is commonly known as a "coconut"- brown Filipino on the outside and white American on the inside. I had to virtually rewire my thinking to fit my new environment, so while I look Filipino, I now think and behave like an American.

Becoming a "coconut" was never what I envisioned as a result of entering the American "melting pot." This metaphor is commonly applied to the United States and it describes a society where people of different ethnic backgrounds blend together as one.

Originally, I thought the phrase "melting pot" meant that the dominant taste inside the metaphorical pot was determined by the various cultural components blended inside. As more cultural ingredients were added to the mix, theoretically, the flavor would have to change accordingly.

However, my experience taught me that the opposite was true. The flavor in the pot was already predetermined, and in this case, it was unmistakably American. By jumping into the theoretical melting pot, I had to shed the taste of my Filipino customs and gradually absorbed the dominant American flavor. Hence, I emerged from the melting pot as a changed man, a "coconut."

Although I've assimilated exceptionally well to American culture, there is a small part of my Filipino heritage that will always remain in me. If I were to quantify how American I've become, conservatively, I would estimate myself to be about 90% American and 10% Filipino.

I lived the first 15 years of my life in an environment where people like me were the majority. I know how it feels to belong to a homogeneous society where everyone looks like me, acts like me, and adheres to the same culture. In such an environment, there was a level of comfort and security inherent to being part of the larger majority. Now that I no longer live in my native land, and despite the fact that I've integrated so well in the American culture, I don't quite feel that same sensation of 100% sense of cultural belonging I once had. On the other hand, after being away for so long, whenever I visit the Philippines, I no longer have that feeling there either.

I'm in a cultural limbo, stuck between two cultures like the hyphen between the words "Filipino-American." Not surprisingly, this "hyphen" feeling is a common peculiarity shared by all of the expatriates I've gotten to know. However, when I share these distinctions to my American acquaintances, I often get rebuffed and lectured why I shouldn't feel that way. Some of them genuinely tried to learn and understand my position, but there are those who couldn't get past their opinionated views and insisted for me to, "Get over it."

What these individuals clearly failed to understand is that I don't necessarily view my being in a "hyphen" state as a bad thing. In fact, I consider it to be an advantage for reasons that the world today is far more intertwined than ever before. A strong argument can be made that in today's highly connected world, with its exceedingly mobile inhabitants, multi-cultural integration is inevitable. With globalization in full swing, it plays out perfectly for expatriates like me who are multi-lingual, adaptable to cultural changes, and works well with people from diverse ethnic background. From a vantage point of view, I consider being a "hyphen-man" as strength, not a weakness.

Another prevailing attitude amongst my American friends on the subject of cultural awareness has been, "Immigrants choose to come to this country, and it is their responsibility to adjust to the American way, not the other way around."

It may be true and such mind-set may not pose any harm when applied to mere acquaintances, or to those whose existence does not affect us in any way. However, such dismissive views may not bode well when dealing with an important client or a business partner who happens to be of a different cultural back ground. As I had alluded to previously, an encounter of this sort is not uncommon in major cities, such as Los Angeles, where a mosaic of cultural diversity exists. It is worth repeating that in such an environment, familiarity in cultural etiquette may serve to one's advantage, at the very least one ought to know which cultural buttons not to push.

The other judgment call I often come across is that the American culture must be better than the Filipino culture, since I choose to make the United States my home. I've heard this generalized conclusion so often that it doesn't even faze me anymore like it used to. What I have discovered in my long journey is that cultural differences are neither good nor bad, they're just different. And different doesn't mean it's wrong, just because it might not be right for me, doesn't mean it's not right for someone else.

Vesting the time to understand, learn, and respect each other's culture, is what fosters my awareness, tolerance, and cooperation from other people. Being culturally aware makes me less inclined to take offense to behaviors that are different from mine. It reminds that they may just be using cultural expressions and behaviors they are comfortable with and not necessarily acting out of malice, ignorance, or indifference.

These days, when I return to the Philippines, I often find myself wandering along the open farmer's market where Grandma Rufina used to take me in my childhood. As I made my way through the maze of colorful stalls, I can't help but wished Grandma was walking beside me. I imagined how wonderful it would be for her to freely point at any goodies she wanted without having to concern herself with affordability. Her priceless reaction would be a treasure to see. I was all she had, but she unselfishly let me go so I may have a better chance in life. I can't even imagine how much strength and courage it took for her to let go of the one person who mattered most to her.

Grandma passed away on February 15th, 1981, and Grandpa Antonio followed one month later. His lifeless body was discovered on the same spot where, years ago, he and I spent the night on the ledge of an old radio station. The only possession found with him was a wallet containing that same old faded photograph of him and Grandma Rufina. He carried that picture with him to the end; a trace of a lifelong pursuit for a love that was never meant to be. For better or for worse, to him, Grandma Rufina was all that ever mattered.

In 2007, Uncle Inar and I sought to find Grandpa Antonio's grave. I wanted to place his remains in a chamber together with Grandma Rufina's. Reuniting their remains, I felt, was the least I could do to atone for what the two of them could not attain in life.

My uncle and I searched the cemetery for most of the day, but to no avail. We consulted the cemetery's administrative office, and learned that after three years of missed payments, the cemetery's policy was to remove the remains of the deceased to make room for other burials. My grandfather's remains had probably been dug up long ago and simply tossed aside. Despite the discouraging news, Uncle Inar and I continued our search through the rest of the afternoon on the off chance that we would still find Grandpa Antonio's forgotten grave. Unfortunately, we never did.

Uncle Segundo was the first of my three uncles to pass on. His long battle with asthma eventually took its toll. He called me on the phone a few days after the 9/11 terrorist attack in 2001, to inquire if everyone in the family was alright. His call came in at 3 a.m., I was still half asleep and had to, unfortunately, cut his call short. I saw him last the year before his death. He walked me to my taxi and as he reached over to open the car door, Uncle said to me, "God willing, we will see each other again next year, kid."

I replied jokingly, "Just don't die on me, man. Whatever happens, just keep breathing until I get back. Alright?"

As he closed the door, his parting words to me were, "I will, kid. You bet I will."

Uncle Segundo died on May 15th, 2002. He was sixty two.

Amazingly, my Uncle Anastacio lived beyond his six-year prison term and well into his seventies. On October 8th, 2011, his life of drunkenness finally did him in. He was extremely inebriated when he tripped, cracked his head open, and bled to death.

I had always envisioned that hearing of his demise would be the happiest moment of my life. To my surprise, when the word did finally arrive, my reaction was not at all what I had expected. For days, all I could think of was the handful of pleasant memories I had with him. I thought of the time when he made me a colorful kite that flew perfectly still the moment it took off the ground. I recalled evenings around the dinner table, when he was sober, and would tell me stories about the fighting roosters he had previously owned. Hatred was the furthest thing from my mind.

From the time I visited him in prison in 1990 to the day of his passing, I never had any worthwhile conversations with Anastacio. He'd always hit me up for money whenever I was in the neighborhood, and I'd give him a few pesos. That was the extent of our contact until my next visit, when he'd ask for money again. The only conversation I had of any meaningful significance with him was in 2010, when I asked him if he remembered anything about his real father. Uncle was a bit tipsy and belligerent, but he was no longer the physical threat he once was. With a tone of pride resonating in his voice, he replied, "The day my father died was the happiest day of my life."

Anastacio then went on and on about the beatings he received from his father. He tried to convince me that he was only a product of his environment, and cowardly placed the blame of his own misdeeds on someone else's shoulder. This man subjected me to the same cruelty inflicted upon him by his father. I could have used Anastacio as an excuse to argue that I, too, was a product of my environment - but I know better. I alone am responsible for my own actions. I've never forgotten the pain and suffering Anastacio brought into my life. I still remember those countless evenings when Grandma would cry herself to sleep next to me.

In years of encounters with Anastacio, he never once apologized or expressed remorse for the pain he caused Grandma and me. Instead of embroiling myself with hatred for this man, I simply moved on long ago and put my energy to better use. His influence just didn't matter to me anymore.

The great irony of it all was that I ended up paying for Anastacio's funeral expenses. I didn't even like the guy. But if I hadn't, Uncle Inar would have ended up footing the bill. I didn't want that to happen, so I ended up being the one who buried the man I once hated with a passion.

From a child's perspective, I had known my Uncle Inar to be a dreamer and hard worker. I still remember him in the sugar cane fields, chopping away and dreaming big dreams that were far too high for his reach. Forever etched in my memory was the image of Uncle Inar working endlessly, alone in his field of dreams. He worked with a sense of urgency, as if his dream of a better life could be reached at the end of his allotted track.

Sadly, it would take years of back breaking work for him to discover that no matter how many acres he cleared away in a given day, there would always be endless plots to cover. The vast sugar cane field was meant for someone like Uncle Inar to get lost in, not to rise out of.

In retrospect, I found it ironic that in a culture that highly priced compassion and altruism; some wealthy land owners find it necessary to exploit the poor and the uneducated. Apparently, greed knows no cultural boundaries.

The reality of Uncle Inar's existence had long ago snuffed the burning determination I had once seen in his eyes. When I saw him again years later, he was a broken man. The crushing weight of his hopeless situation had gotten the best of him and he had succumbed to alcoholism. Uncle Inar's drinking ultimately led to his demise.

I saw him last in December, 2011. We made plans to take a trip to his former home on the island of Negros in my next visit.

Unfortunately, he passed away on January 29th, 2012, before I could make it back to see him. He was sixty-two years old.

As of this writing, my parents are still alive and well. They still live in the home they purchased back in 1976. It's the family's main gathering venue for holidays and special occasions. They now have thirteen grandchildren and ten great-grandchildren. Dad's eyes still retains the intense glow of a man in love. In this life, he has truly found his better half in Mom.

My daughters, Rena and Niah, have blossomed into beautiful, mature, and responsible women. I set across the table from them during our weekly lunch date, where I get the sheer pleasure of hearing them carry on with conversations about new challenges and surprises they uncover each day in this thing called life.

Although Grandma did not live long enough to see what became of the little boy she had lovingly protected, nurtured, and raised. She'd be pleased to know that her love and sacrifices were not in vain. In some small way, I've tried to live my life in a manner that she could be proud of; someone others could look at and see themselves in. If she could only see me today, Grandma Rufina would be proud of the man I've become.

Sharing these experiences in writing fills me with nostalgia for my humble beginning in the Philippines and the rough cultural assimilation I experienced in America. This journey has given me a greater understanding that, indeed, cultural differences matter: How profoundly they differ and powerful these differences can be.

The road to cultural integration is never going to be easy. It is my hope that sharing my experience will be of help to immigrants as they venture and navigate their way into the cultural maze of the great unknown. It is also my aspiration to bring about the general awareness that there is far more to an immigrant than meets the eye.

In life absolute certainty is a rarity, but the one thing I'm certain of is that as human beings, we learn, we adapt, and we evolve.

Mother and I, 1961.

A family portrait: (From left) my uncles, Inar Barrientos, Segundo Sanchez, Anastacio Sanchez, (Seated from left) my mother, Yolanda Sanchez, and my grandmother, Rufina Cabreros, 1966.

My sister Gina and I, 1966.

Mother and Dad (my stepfather, Willard "Bill" Long) on their wedding day, 1966.

My sister Gina and I along with our friends, celebrating my 7th birthday in Alumnos..

My step grandfather, Antonio Barrientos (1911-1981).

Grandma Rufina Cabreros (1912-1981).

ACKNOWLEDGEMENTS

I am particularly grateful to Andrea Chita and Jean Ardell for their editorial guidance and valuable contributions. I also wanted to express my deep gratitude to Doug Clak and Christine Padua-Lopez for their kind words of encouragement when needed most.